Learning with the Brain in Mind

Learning with the Brain in Mind

Frank McNeil

Los Angeles • London • New Delhi • Singapore • Washington DC

First published 2009

Apart from any fair dealing for the purposes
of research or private study, or criticism or
review, as permitted under the Copyright,
Designs and Patents Act, 1988, this publication
may be reproduced, stored or transmitted in any
form, or by any means, only with the prior
permission in writing of the publishers, or in the
case of reprographic reproduction, in accordance
with the terms of licences issued by the Copyright
Licensing Agency. Enquiries concerning
reproduction outside those terms should be
sent to the publishers.

SAGE Publications Ltd
1 Oliver's Yard
55 City Road
London EC1Y 1SP

SAGE Publications Inc.
2455 Teller Road
Thousand Oaks, California 91320

SAGE Publications India Pvt Ltd
B 1/I 1 Mohan Cooperative Industrial Area
Mathura Road
New Delhi 110 044

SAGE Publications Asia-Pacific Pte Ltd
33 Pekin Street #02-01
Far East Square
Singapore 048763

Library of Congress Control Number 2008927067

British Library Cataloguing in Publication data

A catalogue record for this book is available from
the British Library

ISBN 978-1-4129-4525-7
ISBN 978-1-4129-4526-4 (pbk)

Typeset by C&M Digitals (P) Ltd, Chennai, India
Printed in India at Replika Press Pvt Ltd
Printed on paper from sustainable resources

Contents

Contents

Foreword

Until now education systems have been designed with little under-standing of how the human brain works. Teaching has been under-taken with only the vaguest knowledge of how humans actually learn. Our knowledge of the brain has been acquired from autopsies and medical treatments involving invasive brain surgery. This situa-tion, however, is changing. One of the most exciting developments in medicine today involves a growing understanding of our most complex organ and an unravelling of how the mind might work.

Frank McNeil trained as a school teacher in the early 1960s, after a career in the Royal Navy. He came as a student on teaching practice to my classroom in south London. Since then, I have watched him develop as a teacher, a head teacher, an inspector and an educational researcher. In all these years and in these different roles he has main-tained a sense of wonder and, committed teacher that he is, the determination to pass on his knowledge and enthusiasm.

In this book, McNeil introduces his readers to the developing science of scanning and takes them on a journey around the brain. He describes the billions of neurons, axons and dendrites that enable us to give attention to objects and ideas, to remember information and to learn new skills. In arguing that the ability to focus in a sustained way is fundamental to human development, he touches on the cru-cial need to pay attention – as demanded by teachers of their pupils throughout the centuries.

McNeil is not afraid to be controversial. He warns parents of the dan-gers of letting young children watch too much television and even of not getting enough sleep. He also enters the debate about how the emotions are linked to intellectual development.

Drawing on his long experience in the education system, McNeil identifies many teaching opportunities, identifies further sources of information and inspires interest in these unfolding developments. As he notes, the time lag between neuroscientists discovering how the brain works, and teachers and schools adopting new methods better to support learning, is bound to be sizeable. But, as with the massive GNOME project, scientists will eventually complete their work and the baton will be passed on to teachers. Reading this book will help prepare them to take up this all-important challenge.

Peter Mortimore

Acknowledgements

Grateful thanks to Angela Sheahan of Highlands Primary School, Redbridge who has been most generous with her time in poring over drafts and offering guidance. Thanks also to Clare McNeil for her encouragement and valuable suggestions. And my final thanks must go to Helen Fairlie and Rachel Hendrick from Sage for their patient help.

Introduction

I read my first book about the brain when I was a school inspector, and I immediately wanted to read all that I could understand about neuroscience and brain studies. The reason for this compulsion was because my time as a teacher was plagued by notions of learning as a set of polarised arguments – 'look-say *v* phonics', 'progressive *v* traditional' and other dichotomies. These debates created something of a battleground, where both pupils and their teachers were the losers. As I read more about the brain, I realised that our understanding of learning could one day be partly based on science, as the evidence from neuroscience would provide the datum for a science of learning. This could lead to a broad consensus as to what learning is about and enable teachers to enjoy more public support for their work.

The nineties of course was the decade of the brain and there were great expectations developing as to what brain studies might offer in the future. However, at present the evidence from neuroscience that informs learning is like a huge and only partly-formed Roman mosaic; incomplete yet fascinating. New research about the brain is coming in thick and fast, and in time I am convinced it will have a powerful influence on theories of learning. Already there are major strands of evidence that are having an impact by creating a sea change in our understanding of how learning evolves and develops through our earliest experiences. This book aims to investigate how our understanding of learning, and therefore of teaching, is changing.

The quality of an individual's life, and therefore to some extent the quality of life in society, is directly linked to the experience of love, supervision and support of early childhood. The foundations of learning and intellectual development are established at the same time and from the same roots. Evidence from brain studies is helping us to understand how children grow, learn and develop from dependent infants to fully functioning adults. It is becoming clear that successful adults owe a great deal to their thoughtful and caring parents and other caregivers, and studying the brain in the earliest stages of life sheds light on why this may be so. A major theme of this book is that formal schooling should as far as possible be married to the experience, skills, knowledge and talents that children bring into school with them.

The structure of the book

Learning with the Brain in Mind describes how learning evolves, develops and is sustained from the earliest stages of life, and how teaching in particular ways can enhance this process. The book is structured around three chapters reflecting the three major learning themes of attention, the emotions, and memory. Another three supporting chapters look at brain scanning, the structure of the brain and the social brain with wellbeing in school.

Chapter 1, 'Seeing inside the brain', describes the main scanning techniques that enable us to observe, and sometimes to measure, changes in brain activity. It is important to appreciate the nature and value of the evidence where learning is concerned – the technology is developing rapidly and it may not be too fanciful to envisage that in the future some children will come to school with scans of their brains to assist their teaching.

Chapter 2, 'A journey round the brain', provides basic information about the geography of the brain and the main functions of the various regions, with a focus on the synapses where learning is thought to take place. This short chapter is intended as a reference source for the other chapters in providing explanations of technical terms, and may also be useful as a basis for teaching pupils about their brains.

Chapter 3, 'Pay attention and get connected!', focuses on the theme of attention, and is the first of the three major and interconnected chapters about learning. Using evidence from neuroscience, it argues that attention should be regarded as the foundation skill for learning, and that it should be supported, encouraged and in some cases taught from the earliest stages of life.

Chapter 4, 'Learning and the emotions', explains how the emotions are not only essential to the formation of the brain, but also how they are fundamental to learning at all stages of life.

Chapter 5, 'Memory, the brain and learning', argues that memory grows from early experience, that there are differences between experts and novices and that memory strategies can and should be taught.

The themes of chapters 3, 4 and 5, namely, Attention, Emotions and Memory, form the triangle of learning referred to frequently in the book.

Chapter 6, 'The social brain', addresses the concept of brain plasticity (how the brain is constantly changing in response to experience) which recurs throughout the book. The social aspects of learning are considered, and suggestions are made about how pupils' views of their experience could be taken into account in order to improve the quality of life and learning in school.

I remember as a teacher periods of laissez-faire in schools where teachers were largely left to themselves, to the disadvantage of many pupils. However I feel the pendulum has swung too far in the other direction, to the point where many teachers feel they are just implementing others' ideas and theories of learning. Sadly, some teachers also feel they are not able to learn from their own experience with pupils and develop their own pedagogy.

I hope this book will provide practitioners and those others interested in the emerging evidence from neuroscience with an understanding of the possibilities for the future of learning and therefore of schools.

1

Seeing inside the brain

With the advent of brain scanning in the past twenty-five years, there has been nothing short of a revolution in our understanding of the brain. This brief chapter will describe the main forms of brain scanning that provide the basis for much of the evidence referred to in this book. Here you will learn more about:

- the principal forms of brain scanning;

- the evidence that is produced by different forms of scanning techniques;

- some possibilities for what we might learn to help pupils in the future and particularly those with special needs.

The context – two quotes

The following quotations suggest why scanning is important for our understanding of both the nature of the brain and of learning in the future. The first is from the neuroscientist and author Steven Rose:

> From physics and engineering come the new windows into the brain offered by the imaging systems: PET, fMRI, MEG and others – acronyms which conceal powerful machines offering insights into the dynamic electrical flux through which the living brain conducts its millisecond by millisecond business. (Rose, 2005)

The second is from the project on 'Learning Sciences and Brain Research' in the Organization for Economic Co-operation and Development.

As with most advances in science, the key is the development of new technology. Techniques such as functional neuro-imaging, including functional Magnetic Resonance Imaging (fMRI) and Positron emission tomography (PET) together with Transcranial Magnetic Stimulation (TMS) are enabling scientists to understand more clearly the workings of the brain and the nature of the mind. In particular they can begin to shed new light on old questions about human learning and suggest ways in which educational provision and the practice of teaching can better help young and adult learners. (OECD, 2002)

In light of this comment from the OECD, it is possible to argue that more has been learned about the human brain in the past twenty five-years than in the whole of previous history because of the non-invasive techniques of brain scanning.

We are at the beginning of an era of brain information that will have many implications for teachers and learners. Brain studies will become an essential element of training for teachers, and I would argue that it should already be on the students' curriculum also. In the final chapter regarding the wellbeing of pupils in schools, the issue of the effects upon the brain of taking substances will be considered. Evidence from brain scans should play in important part in this debate.

Looking into the past

Neuroscience emerged at the interface between medicine, psychology and philosophy. As Steven Rose points out, its earliest rationale must have been in the attempts to treat or mitigate overt brain damage, presumably caused by head injuries. He notes that 'trepanning' – that is, making holes in or cutting out sections of the cranium – was practised by the Egyptians and 'maybe goes back much earlier if the surgical marks on prehistoric skulls found widely distributed across Europe are anything to go by' (Rose, 2005). This practice was not confined to the West. In fact it was more widespread in the ancient world, for as he notes, 10,000 trepanned skulls were found in Cuzco in Peru!

The problem for earlier civilisations was that until the advent of microscopy it was difficult to observe much of the structure of the brain beyond the division of white and grey tissues and the curious doubling of the hemispheres. So the Greek philosophers Plato and Hippocrates agreed that the heart was the seat of the emotions and the brain just balanced body heat. The seventeenth century philosopher

Descartes proposed that the brain was like a machine and insisted that the mind and the body were entirely separate.

Some two hundred years later the German physiologist Johannes Muller showed that the perception of the senses takes place in the brain when he demonstrated that each of the sensory organs responds to stimuli in its own way:

> So, if the optic nerve leading from the eye to the brain is stimulated, we see a flash of light regardless of whether the light was the stimulus. (Greenfield, 1996)

Yet despite this emerging scientific understanding, the curious and sometimes dubious art of phrenology survived well into the twentieth century. Phrenology is based on the notion that the mind is intimately related to physical brain function. Hence phrenologists would feel the shape of the head, and the bumps that reflected supposed traits of ability and character, in order to give a reading. I remember as a child hearing about a relation who had had 'his bumps read'.

Present day practice

The revolution in diagnostic imaging that led to the wide range of safe practices that are available today began as recently as the 1970s. Early in this decade, the medical world was introduced to a remarkable imaging technique known formally as X-ray Computed Tomography, now usually termed X-ray CT. This technique passes a beam of x-rays through the tissue at many different angles in a selected plane. The result looks rather like a sliced section through the body. The computer was needed to process the vast amount of information that was necessary to create the actual images.

The impact of this work was twofold. First, it avoided the need for radiological examinations which were unpleasant and sometimes dangerous for patients, and second it opened up fresh possibilities for scientists with new ways of imaging the body 'using the same basic mathematical and computer strategies for image reconstruction' (Posner, 1999).

PET scans
The next major change to follow X-ray CT was Positron Emission Tomography, or PET scans for short. This is a nuclear technique that

produces an image of the distribution of radioactivity in the human body following the administration of a substance containing radioactive atoms. The resulting pictures are in vivid colour, with the lightest colours reflecting the areas of greatest brain activity. My first encounter with PET scans was in 1994, when watching the Christmas television lectures for children delivered by Susan Greenfield. She demonstrated which parts of the brain were active during activities such as reading out loud, working out numerical problems and reading silently. Although the scans didn't yield a great deal of information, they provided a fascinating insight into the brain and were an interesting indicator of where the work might be heading in the future.

A celebrated study using PET scanning showed the plasticity of the adult brain. (Maguire et al., 1997). In this study, London taxi drivers of many years' experience were scanned while they recalled complex routes around the city, and the results were compared with a control group. It was found that the posterior hippocampi of the taxi drivers were significantly larger than those of the control subjects, and that the hippocampal volume correlated with the amount of time spent as a taxi driver. Clearly, the taxi drivers had elaborated their spatial representation of the environment as adults, reflecting the plasticity of the adult brain.

MRI – Magnetic Resonance Imaging

The next major technique to be developed was Magnetic Resonance Imaging or MRI. This approach exploits the fact that many atoms in the presence of a magnetic field behave like little bar magnets or compass needles. By skilfully manipulating the atoms in a magnetic field, scientists can line up the atoms just as the needle of a compass lines up in the earth's magnetic field. When radio wave pulses are applied to a sample whose atoms have been so aligned, the sample will emit detectable radio signals that are characteristic of the number of particular atoms present and of their chemical environment. The resultant images of organ anatomy provide much better detail than the two earlier procedures.

Benefits of fMRI scans

A further development led to the process often used today and known as functional Magnetic Resonance Imaging or fMRI. It uses MRI to capture the quick, tiny metabolic changes that take place in an active part of the brain: 'Essentially fMRI shows up the areas where there is most oxygen' (Carter, 1998). In routine practice, fMRI studies are frequently used in planning brain surgery, since it can help physicians to monitor normal brain functions as well as any disturbed patterns. Currently it appears that fMRI can also help to assess the effects of stroke, trauma or degenerative disease. The conventional fMRI unit is a cylindrical magnet in which the patient must lie still for several seconds at a time, and it can feel claustrophobic to some (especially children, one might imagine).

fMRI images of the brain and other head structures are clearer and more detailed than those obtained by other methods. The medical applications are still developing, and include:

- identifying the location of normal brain function in order to allow surgeons to attempt avoiding these areas during brain surgery;

- enabling the detection of a stroke at a very early stage so physicians can initiate effective treatments;

- helping physicians to monitor the growth and function of brain tumours to guide the planning of radiation therapy or surgical treatment.

Scanning jugglers

There are wider applications of fMRI scanning that yield some evidence about learning. For example, a study at the University of Regensburg using fMRI explored the changes that took place in the brain while volunteers were juggling. Researchers split 24 students into two groups, one of which was given three months to learn a classic three ball cascade juggling routine, the other was a control group. When the jugglers had acquired enough skill to perform for at least a minute, brain scans were carried out on both sets of volunteers.

The scans revealed an increase in grey matter in the visual regions of the brains of the jugglers. In particular, the posterior hippocampi of the jugglers were significantly larger than those of the control subjects. However, after another three months without juggling, the amount of extra grey matter in the jugglers' brains had diminished. This evidence contributes to our understanding of the brain's plasticity, as it shows how the structure of the brain alters in response to environmental demands (Draganski, 2004). The researchers explained that the effect could be due to increased cell production or changes in the connections between neurons.

Electroencephalography (EEG) – electrical recordings of the brain

Techniques that we have encountered so far such as PET and MRI have the potential to enlighten us about where the activity is occurring in the brain while it is performing various tasks. What is not available from these methods alone is the duration of activity in the active areas and the sequence of their activation. Neurons communicate in only milliseconds, but 'it requires about forty seconds to obtain the data necessary to construct a PET image of blood flow in the human brain' (Posner and Raichle, 1999). Therefore, in order to capture the moment-to-moment changes in activity in the brain, scientists turned to other methods, particularly electroencephalography (EEG).

EEG technique 'measures brainwaves – the electrical patterns created by the rhythmic oscillations of neurons' (Carter, 1998). These waves show characteristic changes according to the type of brain activity that is taking place. EEG measures these waves by picking up signals via electrodes placed in the skull. As Posner explains:

> Using geodesic electrode nets, we have examined the effects of tasks similar to those used in PET studies, such as the presentation of visual words. So for example if we want to know when the brain first distinguishes between words and consonant strings, we can compare the wave forms recorded at each of sixty-four electrode sites and find out when they begin to depart from each other. (Posner and Raichle, 1999)

An EEG then, is a recording of signals from the brain made by hooking up electrodes to the subject's scalp. The main drawback of EEG is that it provides less spatial resolution than PET scans. The biggest advantage is speed, since EEG can record complex patterns of neural activity occurring within the brain as soon as a stimulus has been administered. Another significant advantage is that it can be used with children, and there is an increasing number of university and other centres around the world focusing on various aspects of the development of the infant's brain using this technique.

Baby labs and geodesic brain hats

These infant brain research centres, often termed 'Babylabs', are yielding a great deal of information that is important to our understanding of the learning process. One of the best known centres is Birkbeck's Centre for Brain and Cognitive Development, where they focus on how babies learn and develop during the first two years of life. They also study atypical patterns of mental development as seen, for example, in autism. In particular, Birkbeck has focused on the themes of:

- how babies recognise faces;

- how they learn to pay attention to some things and not to others;

- how they learn to understand what other people do and think;

- how their language and understanding of the world develop;

- why and how some children develop disorders such as autism.

The researchers in the centres commonly use a geodesic hairnet which fits over the infant's head and has 64 points of contact on the scalp to provide the EEG information.

A brief survey of some of the infant 'Babylab' study centres around the world found the following themes being researched and studied.

- Cornell, USA: the development of communication, cognition and language;

- Western Sydney, Australia: how infants perceive speech from its vowels to its tones, how infants listen to music, and whether infants are attuned to the 'Aussie' accent;

- Lincoln, UK: categorisation and conceptual development, speech perception, language acquisition, word learning and early grammar;

- Oxford, UK: early word learning, visual perceptual development and understanding of the world of objects;

- Stanford, USA: the origins of communication in infancy and early childhood and how young children develop competence in understanding spoken language;

- Uppsala, Sweden: identifying early deficits in social behaviour, children who are neurologically at risk, and autistic disorders.

This is not a systematic review, but it does indicate the range and depth of the early learning studies taking place with EEG and other scanning technologies. As these develop, they will yield even more evidence about the early stages of life and the acquisition of skills that will inform provision for child care and early learning.

When this evidence is coupled with that from neuro-scientific research centres at universities across the globe, we have a picture of a huge evidence-base that is only possible because of the non-invasive techniques of scanning that are currently in use. The priority now is that of harnessing these findings and disseminating them to those who need such information – not least parents and teachers.

Research using brain scanning

The following examples of brain scanning show particular relevance for learning and indicate the quality and range of evidence that is developing through scanning techniques. They also show the huge value of the emerging evidence-base about learning and important related social issues across the globe.

Some differences between learning Chinese and English

The first example is cross-cultural and from San Diego University. The title is 'How Chinese language and learning pathways differ from alphabet-based languages like English'. In this experiment, the researchers worked with 16 Beijing schoolchildren who were ten to twelve years-old. Eight were dyslexic and the rest were normal readers. The children took turns being placed in an MRI machine as sets of Chinese characters were flashed electronically on a screen. They saw the characters briefly and had to choose an answer by pressing a key with their index finger. During the test, the MRI took snapshots of oxygen-rich blood flowing to the portions of their brain in action.

The results of the study suggest that the brains of Chinese school-children with reading problems misfire in a different region from the one used in reading alphabet-based languages like English. This demonstrates that the learning disorder dyslexia is not the same in every culture and therefore does not have a universal biological cause. Neurologists described these results as 'very important and innovative'. They assert that while dyslexia has certain common roots, they now have proof that this kind of functional problem plays out differently according to the particular demands that western and eastern languages place on the brain's wiring and processing centres.

This kind of study is possible only through the use of scanning technology and it has led to more recent research on a connected theme: 'Dyslexia in Chinese: Thinking in Tongues' (Mossman, *Neuroscience*, January 2007). The original study here is Siok, 2004.

Supporting premature babies

The second study, by researchers at Imperial College, concerns a new test that can identify premature babies who are at risk of developing learning difficulties. The study used MRI scans to measure the brain growth of 113 babies born between 22 and 29 weeks gestation – a baby is normally born at 40 weeks. The babies were scanned up to the point where they would have been eight weeks old if born at full term. The mental development of 63 of the children was then assessed when they were aged about two.

The research showed that the slower the rate of growth of brain surface and the smoother it was compared with brain volume, the more likely it was for a child's development to be delayed. The most premature babies and boys were most likely to be affected.

If the results are confirmed in future studies, the researchers say that it might be possible to use brain scans to identify which children might need development support and even trial treatments. The director of the study, Dr David Edwards, said, 'Now we know what we are looking for, we can try a treatment. We are looking at using melatonin, which is a powerful neuro-protector'. This work could be of great importance for the future of some premature babies (see Kappelou, 2006).

Memory competence in old versus young

A third example investigates factors affecting learning in older adults. The study from Toronto University considers 'The relation between brain activity during memory tasks and years of education in young and older adults'. It is well established that those who experience higher education suffer less age-related decline in cognitive function, but little is known about the mechanism for the protective effect. The research team examined the effect of age on the relation between education and brain activity by correlating years of education with activity measured using functional MRI during memory tasks in young and older adults. In the younger adults, education was negatively correlated with frontal brain activity, whereas in older adults education was positively correlated with frontal activity. The team suggest that the frontal cortex is engaged by older adults, particularly by the highly educated, as an alternative network that may be engaged to aid cognitive function. So, the team conclude that education protects memory by contributing to flexible mental strategies.

Again, this is a rich field of interest and studies in this area are still developing at Toronto University (Grady, 2005).

A two-stage model of learning

The final and most recent example concerns the actual nature of learning and involves the use of advanced imaging techniques with fMRI. The researchers at Georgetown University studied how humans use both higher and lower brain processes to learn novel tasks (see Riesenhuber et al., 2007).

The team provided the first evidence for a two-stage model of how a person learns to place objects into categories. They showed how we can discriminate between a green apple and a green ball, and assign only the apple to the category of food. They describe the process as a complex interplay between neurons: those that recognise and process the basic shapes and other more sophisticated brain areas that discriminate between these shapes to categorise and label that information – a mixture of 'bottom-up' and 'top-down'.

The researchers theorised that a very simple yet efficient way of doing this kind of learning would be for the brain to first learn how objects vary in shape and then in a second stage to learn which shapes go with which labels. So for example, a green apple and a green tennis ball are both round, but the apple can be eaten while the ball belongs to a sport.

The team therefore asked volunteers to undertake a series of tasks presented to them on a computer screen. All of the tasks involved cars that were generated by a computer graphics morphing system that allowed the researchers to generate thousands of cars with subtle shape differences. In the beginning, all of the cars looked very similar because the participants did not have any experience with sorting them.

In the first experiment, the participants looked at series of cars presented in different parts of the screen and produced simple judgements about the positions of particular images. At the same time their brain activity was measured using an advanced fMRI technique that made it possible to more directly probe neuronal tuning than in previous studies. Researchers found that the cars activated a particular region in the participants' brains, namely the lateral occipital cortex, which had also been found by other studies to be important for object recognition.

Then the volunteers were given several hours of training using images of the cars. In these sessions, participants had to learn how to group the cars into two distinct categories. This was easy at first, because the cars were obviously not alike, but as the experiment progressed the researchers made the task more difficult by making the two categories increasingly similar. Over the course of the training, the participants got better at finer category discriminations.

Once the volunteers had learned how to categorise small shape changes, they were shown the cars from the first experiment while again being scanned. This allowed the researchers to compare how training had enhanced the brain's ability to process car shapes. They found again that the cars selectively activated an area in the lateral occipital cortex, but that now neurons in that area appeared to be finely tuned to small car shape differences.

During a third and final scan, the investigators asked subjects to categorise the same car images shown in the other scans. This time two areas of the brain, the now-familiar area of the occipital cortex as well as an area of the lateral pre-frontal cortex, were found to be active when processing the images. The lateral pre-frontal cortex is known to be the centre of cognitive control. It is where the brain connects physical input to an action or response, deciding what task to do and how to respond to a stimulus. In essence then, the fMRI showed that both the higher and lower brain regions had worked together to learn the task. The research team now hope that the findings will be helpful in understanding disorders such as autism or schizophrenia that involve differences in the interaction of bottom-up and top-down information in the brain.

It is clear then that the new scanning technologies are helping us to gain new insights into the functioning of the brain and in some cases to enhance our understanding of the learning process. There is cause for optimism that the vast amount of work taking place in this area will provide us with new and valuable knowledge for pupils with special needs that will also improve the provision for all pupils learning in schools.

Scanning in the future – looking forward

It is certain that the quality and detail of the images from scanning will continue to improve, and that it will be possible to see the brain in action more clearly than current technology allows. In terms of educational applications there should be great strides of progress in our understanding of some aspects of special needs. Some pupils may bring brain scans as part of their educational profile to help the school better understand how to teach them. This will generate its own ethical issues and it will require teachers to have a better understanding of the brain than most do at present. There is likely to be a wealth of information about each student's brain that will be available in the future to support learning. We are at the beginning of an era of brain information that will have many implications for teachers and learners.

Moving objects through brain activity

There are some wonderful possibilities for the future for those pupils who have severe physical disabilities. For example, a new technology from Japan could let pupils control electronic devices without the need for any physical activity. The brain machine interface being developed by a Japanese company analyses slight changes in the brain's blood flow and translates brain motion into electronic signals. A cap, rather like those used by infants in Babylabs and mentioned earlier in this chapter, is connected by optical fibres to a mapping device. This in turn is connected to a computer. Underlying this technology is a process called 'optical topography', which sends a small amount of infra-red light through the brain's surface to map out small changes in blood flow. I saw this demonstrated by a reporter operating a model of an electrical train. As she did small calculations in her brain the train moved forwards, apparently indicating activity in the brain's frontal cortex which handles problem solving. The company has manufactured a device that monitors brain activity in paralysed patients so that they can answer simple questions; for example, by doing mental calculations to indicate 'yes' or thinking of nothing in particular to indicate 'no'. The beauty of this advance is that it is non-invasive and requires only a small helmet, rather than having a chip inserted into the brain.

An altogether different use for brain scanning in the future is already creating an ethical debate. A team of leading neuroscientists at the Max Planck Institute in Germany has developed a powerful technique that allows them to look deep inside a person's brain and to read their intentions before they act. The research breaks controversial new ground, potentially increasing scientists' ability to read the thoughts of others, and raises serious ethical issues about how brain-reading maybe used in the future.

The team used high-resolution brain scans to identify patterns of activity before translating them into meaningful thoughts, revealing what a person is planning to do in the near future. It is the first time that scientists have succeeded in reading intentions in this way. The researchers describe the process as looking around the brain for information 'like shining a torch around and looking for writing on a wall'.

During the study, the researchers asked the volunteers to decide whether to add or subtract two numbers they were later shown on a screen. Before the numbers flashed up they were given a brain scan using fMRI. The researchers then used software that had been designed to spot subtle differences in brain activity to predict the person's intentions with 70 per cent accuracy. The study revealed signatures of activity in a marble-sized part of the brain called the medial prefrontal cortex that changed when a person intended to add the numbers or subtract them. Professor Colin Blakemore, a much respected neuroscientist, noted that these techniques could offer much to education and diagnosis in the future. He also observed that 'we will have more and more ability to probe people's intentions, minds, background thoughts, hopes and emotions' (Sample, 2007).

Patterns of success in chess players

Some ten years ago, Posner and Raichle, both experts in the field of imaging, predicted changes in the future for scanning technologies. They mentioned the work of Herbert Simon, who argued that 50,000 hours or more of practice allows the chess master to develop the highly elaborated semantic memory structure necessary to play at the highest level. This semantic structure allows the master to reproduce, after a mere glance, the more than 30 pieces that occupy the chess board in the middle stages of a master level game. This level of performance far surpasses that of a good chess player, yet the memory of the master for a random chess board configuration or for other kinds of information is only average. Practice has given the chess master a way of representing information that comes into play rapidly and effortlessly. The key question here is: how has the brain of the master changed? Might it be possible for sensitive and non-invasive scanning to illuminate the changes in the brains of experts that would enable others to improve their skills? The answer is almost certainly yes, and it seems only a matter of time before it happens.

Posner and Raichle note that:

> uncovering such developmental changes will help us to address many questions about how the brain acquires and attends to new skills, and the methods used may be applied to discover how adults learn second languages and acquire other types of skill. (Posner and Raichle, 1999)

The aspiration is still that the cognitive study of expertise and the neuro-scientific study of learning will merge to produce new levels of understanding of the relation between brain and mind.

'How beauteous mankind is! O brave new world, That has such people in't' (*The Tempest*, 5.1. 181–183)

One final possibility for the future is suggested in a beautifully illustrated book which seeks an understanding of the mind through the art of Shakespeare and the science of brain imaging (Matthews and McQuain, 2003). Inevitably, in an area of rapid technological growth such as imaging there is the urge to move forward without always referring to and connecting with the past. These writers relate their arguments to Shakespeare, noting that he was concerned not only with the normal brain, but 'he also observed keenly brain diseases which challenge us now'. So, for example, he probed aspects of madness with Hamlet, Ophelia and Lady Macbeth, and with King Lear he addressed the problems of aging and dementia that are so critical in the twenty-first century, while in *Julius Caesar*, he shows how the crowd wondered at Caesar having had a fit in the market square. Shakespeare also observed the way drugs change the mind and behaviour, and these words of Cassio are just as relevant to contemporary society as they were to the Elizabethans:

O, God, that men should put an enemy in their mouths to steal away
their brains! That we should with joy, pleasance, revel and applause,
transform ourselves into beasts! (*Othello*, 2.3. 38)

This book, *The Bard on the Brain*, would be a powerful introduction
for students to the worlds of both Shakespeare and the modern science of brain imaging. One page in particular would hold their
interest, where it shows the juxtaposition of PET scans of normal
brains and those of murderers! Pupils would find the arguments
about diminished responsibility because of poorly functioning
frontal lobes very interesting, rather as Richard III pleads to the
audience that his evil acts are due to his deformities (Matthews and
McQuain, 2003).

There are wonderful images from brain scanning which are easily
found on the web. Here are two books which provide useful and
interesting information on this theme.

Images of Mind – Posner and Raichle (1999)

Although the field of brain imaging has moved on since this prize-
winning book was written, it nevertheless provides a sound background to the techniques of scanning. The authors provide a rich
interpretation of the networks of anatomical areas that become
active during the performance of mental tasks. They provide a
clear visual picture of the ways in which we are beginning to measure human thought processes, while acknowledging that we are
at the beginning of a journey which has yet to include the impact
of multiple assemblies of cells within the brain. The book provides
clear and readable explanations of the foundations of cognitive
neuroscience.

*The Bard on the Brain: Understanding the Brain Through the Art of
Shakespeare and the Science of Brain Imaging* – Matthews and
McQuain (2003)

This wonderful collaboration blends the beauty and mystery of
the human mind with new insights into its workings. The writers
combine 35 beautiful passages from Shakespeare's plays with
images of the brain. The themes are challenging both for teachers
and students. There are sections on 'Minds and Brains' with quotations from *Hamlet* and *The Tempest*, 'Drugs and the Brain' with
Falstaff in praise of alcohol, and Juliet's farewell. A must for any
student of art or science!

2

A journey round the brain

The purpose of this short chapter is to show how the brain works and to illustrate some of the main areas of the brain and their functions. This is intended as a reference point to turn back to when reading other chapters of this book. We begin with the neurons as they are the fundamental elements of the brain.

Neurons – the basic constituents

Here is a wonderful description of the complexity of the brain in action by Nobel Prize winner Gerald Edelman, a highly respected neuroscientist:

> It begins with molecules and goes on to genes. It involves vast numbers of cells with electrical activity and chemical diversity, an enormous intricate anatomy with blobs and sheets linked in rich ways, and maps that receive signals from sensory input and send signals to motor output … All of this comes about as a result of evolution – that is, as a result of natural selection operating over millions of years. (Edelman, 1992)

Edelmann's description eschews the mathematics of the brain where 100 billion neurons have the possibility of communicating with up to 20,000 others, creating what is commonly called the most complex organism in the known universe.

The matter of communication

Our journey begins with the neuron, the essential element of the brain and the basic unit of the nervous system. The neuron has two

Direction of neural Impulse ────────➤

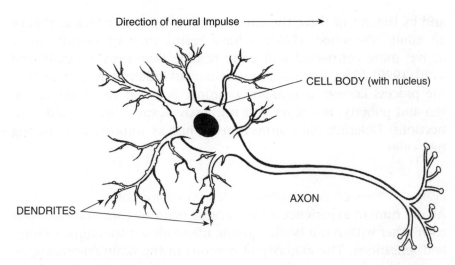

CELL BODY (with nucleus)

AXON

DENDRITES

Figure 2.1   A typical neuron

unique features. The first is that the outer layer is designed to convey nerve signals as electrochemical pulses, and the second is that each cell has projecting parts called dendrites (from the Greek term meaning 'branch') acting mainly as receptors.

Other features of neurons include the axons, which carry signals away from the cell, sometimes a long distance away to other neurons. Many axons have an insulating sheet of myelin, a fatty substance, which helps them to transmit messages faster. Most of the incoming signals to the cell are received by the dendrites which have tiny bumps on them known as dendritic spines. The dendrites are so numerous that they represent 90 per cent or more of the cell's surface.

In addition to the neurons, there are glial cells which have many functions. Mainly they serve to support the neurons, helping to cleanse, carry nutrients and assist in repair. Until recently it was thought that these were their only functions, but there is now the suggestion that they may play a role in intelligence.

Almost all the neurons in the brain are generated well before birth, mainly in the first three months of pregnancy. An adult brain as mentioned previously has around 100 billion brain cells, which is close to the number we are born with. There is something paradoxical here though. Children's brains are actually much busier than ours and by the age of three the child's brain is twice as active as that of an adult: 'Pre-school children have brains that are literally more active, more connected and more flexible than ours' (Gopnik and Kuhl, 1999). Since the brain cannot expand indefinitely, this leads to the process known as synaptic pruning. Between about the age of ten and puberty, the brain will ruthlessly destroy the weakest connections. Deleting old connections is just as important as adding new ones.

How neurons communicate – making connections

All our human experience arises because neurons communicate with each other within our bodies, giving life to all our thoughts, feelings and sensations. The majority of neurons in the brain communicate with each other by means of tiny trickles of signals which are both electrical and chemical.

The electrical currents are not the same as the mechanical currents that we use in our homes. The impulses in the brain are the result of the movement of four common ions – sodium, potassium, calcium and chloride. Sodium, potassium and calcium are positive ions and chloride is negative. Inside the membrane of the neuron, there is an overall excess of negative ions and outside there is an excess of positive ions. Since opposite charges attract, positive and negative ions line up on either side of the membrane. The living cell therefore is like a battery, with the resting neuron holding a slightly negative charge.

When the neuron is stimulated by receiving excitatory signals from another neuron, the sodium channels in the membrane open and the positively charged sodium ions enter the cell. The rise in voltage that is created is known as an action potential. The shift in charge 'as the ions move, is an electrochemical event and produces an electrical pulse – the nerve signal' (Greenfield, 1996).

The synaptic gap

At the next stage of the nerve signal's journey, when the bioelectrical current reaches the terminal of one axon and the junction with the dendrite on the cell body of another neuron, a mystery arises. There is a gap, known as the synaptic gap, between the cells, and the mystery is how the tiny electrical current is translated into a chemical which is fired across it. On the other side of the gap the pulse is

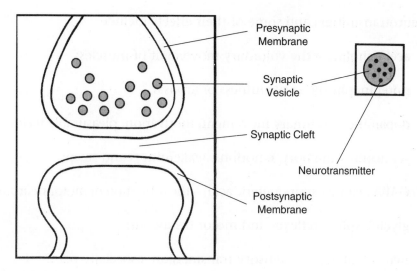

Presynaptic Membrane

Synaptic Vesicle

Synaptic Cleft

Neurotransmitter

Postsynaptic Membrane

Figure 2.2

re-translated and the message continues its journey as a current to the next neuron.

So the plot thickens, since transmission of information between neurons almost always occurs by chemical rather than electrical means. The action potential, the electrical change described above, causes the release of specific chemical agents that are stored in synaptic vesicles. These chemicals, or neurotransmitters, are fired across the synaptic gap and they bind with receptors on the membrane of the receiving neuron. The receptors cause tiny channels in the receiving cell's membrane to open, allowing the charged particles of ions into or out of the cell. This is as near as we may presently get to a description of the actual point of learning, namely the exchange of electricity and chemicals between two neurons.

Neurotransmitters

The chemicals in neurotransmitters are used to relay and amplify the electrical signals between a neuron and another cell. Susan Greenfield says that they act like 'keys that fit into the locks of receptors' (Greenfield, 1996). It is important to appreciate that it is the receptor that dictates the neurotransmitter's effect, rather than where the signal is coming from. The types of neurotransmitter are usually divided into amino acids, peptides and monoamines. Peptides are the focus of the work of Candace Pert, where she explores their role in weaving the body's organs and systems into a single web (Pert, 1997).

Neurotransmitters and some of their effects include:

- acetylcholine – the voluntary movement of muscles;

- norepinephrine – wakefulness or arousal;

- dopamine – voluntary movement, motivation, pleasurable feelings;

- serotonin – memory, emotions, wakefulness and sleep;

- GABA (gamma aminobutyric acid) – the inhibition of motor neurons;

- glycine spinal reflexes and motor behaviour;

- neuromodulators – sensory transmission, especially pain.

A crucial function of neurotransmitters is that they have either an excitatory or inhibitory function, depending on the receptor that they bind to. This means they may either help the initiation of a nerve impulse in the receiving neuron, or they may discourage such an impulse. Glutamate is the most prominent of the excitatory neurotransmitters and GABA (gamma-aminobutryric acid) and glycine are known for their inhibitory functions.

The impact of drugs

Many neurotransmitters are removed from the synaptic cleft (a narrow gap which separates the axon from the post synaptic cell) by neurotransmitter transporters in a process called re-uptake. Without re-uptake, the molecules might continue to stimulate or inhibit the firing of the post synaptic neuron. Where recreational and other drugs are being used, this process can be deliberately inhibited. For example:

- cocaine blocks the re-uptake of dopamine, leaving the neurotransmitters in place for longer;

- Prozac inhibits the uptake of serotonin;

- alcohol decreases the release of GABA;

- heroin and morphine mimic the natural endorphins;

- nicotine activates receptors on the hippocampal cells that typically respond to acetylcholine.

You will find more detailed information about the effe(
the brain in the final chapter of this book. For detailed
of the effects of stress and depression on the brain an
tion with addiction, see *Why Zebras Don't Get Ulcers* (Sa

Brain plasticity through neural networks

One of the key concepts about the brain that is crucial for learning
and views of intelligence is the notion of its plasticity – the capacity
to be modified by experience. As the eminent neuroscientist Gerald
Edelman comments: 'A key property of synapses is that they are plastic'
(Edelman, 2006). The brain is constantly changing with experience,
and it is experiences and usage that shape the brain throughout life.
Hence the adage 'use it or lose it' is as valid for the brain as it is for
the body. The underlying principle behind plasticity was described
more than fifty years ago by the Canadian psychologist D.O. Hebb.
He explained that when one neuron signals to another and the second neuron becomes activated, the connection is strengthened
increasingly as the activation continues. Hence his dictum, 'neurons
that fire together wire together' (Hebb, 1949).

The neuroscientist Sarah Jayne Blakemore sums this up, and comments:

> So not only does the physical structure of the brain change slightly
> with experience, learning also modifies the brain's chemical character-
> istics. Whether this is permanent or not has yet to be verified, but
> clearly for optimal adaptation, not all learning should be permanent.
> (Blakemore and Frith, 2005)

The idea of plasticity is of great importance in considering the learning brain. As we shall see later, the work of the psychologist Carol
Dweck and others challenges the idea of intelligence as a fixed and
predictable capacity. This in turn has significance for pupils.

In his influential work *Synaptic Self* (2002), Joseph Le Doux explains
that most systems of the brain are plastic. However, he considers that
learning is not the function that the systems were originally designed
to perform:

> They were built instead to accomplish certain tasks like detecting dan-
> ger, finding food and mates, hearing sounds. So learning and synaptic
> plasticity are just features that help them to do their job better. (Le
> Doux, 2002)

Learning then has a crucial function in our mechanisms for survival. This is endorsed by Gerald Edelman with his theory of 'Neural Darwinism'. Edelman argues that synapses in the brain, like animals in their environments, compete to stay alive. Synapses that are used compete successfully and survive, while those that are not used perish (Edelman, 2006).

The connections between learning and survival are important when we consider the relevance of the school curriculum for pupils and their attainment. For example, it is clear that speaking and listening are survival skills, and most of us are richly equipped to acquire and use them. Reading and writing, although seen as survival skills in the modern or postmodern world, are not essentially to do with survival in our distant past, and therefore require different approaches to teach them. However, the point is not always understood that reading and writing derive from speaking and listening and thus are built on this foundation. Put another way, listening and speaking need to be well developed before reading and writing can become purposeful and fluent.

Neurogenesis – a recent discovery

Until quite recently, it was thought that the 100 billion brain cells that we are born with was our full complement, notwithstanding the 1000 or so a day that we lose after the age of forty. Ongoing neurogenesis – that is, the birth of new neuronal cells – occurs in the hippocampus and throughout adult life. It is thought to be an important mechanism underlying neuronal plasticity, enabling organisms to adapt to environmental changes and influencing learning and memory for life (Eriksson et al., 1998).

Grey and white matter

The central nervous system is a highly heterogeneous structure in terms of the distribution of nerve cell bodies and their processes. Some regions are relatively rich in the quantity of nerve cell bodies and are referred to as 'grey matter'. Other areas have more nerve processes, usually axons, and these are known as 'white matter'. The paler colour derives from the axons having a coating of myelin which enables the trickles of electricity to travel. The illness of multiple sclerosis occurs when the myelin sheathing begins to break down, with the result that the messages don't always find their way through.

Having seen a little of how neurons communicate, we now move to consider the main areas of the brain and their functions.

The geography of the brain – the principal regions

The cerebrum, which is the Latin term for the whole brain, is like the shape you make when you place your fists together and side by side. The size is similar to that of a coconut. The surface of the cerebrum is covered by the cerebral cortex, which is divided into two hemispheres and joined by the corpus callossum that has approximately 250 million fibres to richly interconnect the two hemispheres. The word 'cortex' derives from the Latin for 'bark' and describes the appearance of the mantle which is convoluted in order to maximise the space, and this is where most of the brain's higher processing takes place. If the cerebral cortex was smooth rather than wrinkled, the brain would have to be the size of a basketball.

1. The frontal lobes

We will follow Figure 2.3 on p.24 in a clockwise direction and start with the frontal lobes. This region is the most recently developed area of the brain in evolutionary terms and controls the functions that most of us would consider make us civilised. Elkhonon Goldberg, a specialist in frontal lobes, explains that their development began to accelerate only with the great apes:

> As the seat of intentionality and foresight and planning, the frontal lobes are the most uniquely human of all the components of the human brain. (Goldberg, 2001)

He calls the pre-frontal cortex the 'Executive Lobe', and says that it acts as the Chief Executive Officer for the rest of the brain:

> The pre frontal cortex plays the central role in forming goals and objectives and then in devising plans of action required to attain these goals.

Similarly, the lobes also select and co-ordinate the cognitive skills to implement plans and to evaluate actions. In a more personal sense they also deal with empathy and altruism – the attitudes that make us civilised and responsive to others.

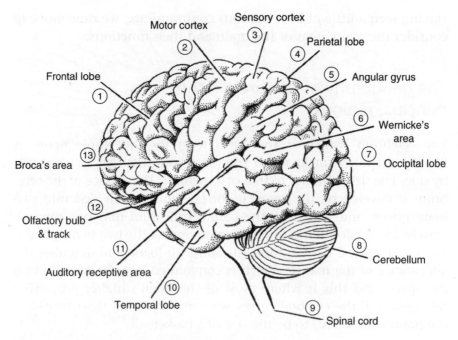

Figure 2.3   Illustration by McKenzie Illustrations

2. The motor cortex

When you decide, say, to pour a glass of water, the directors of the movement process are two strips of grey matter over the top of the brain. These are the left and right motor cortices. The best way to describe the proportions of the brain dedicated to movement is to refer to the motor homonculus – a little man with a body whose proportions indicate the relative amount of the brain used for that function. So the hands, mouth and feet have the largest areas of the cortex, reflecting their importance to us. (Figure 2.4 below)

3. The somato-sensory cortex

In the brain, information about touch arrives at the somato-sensory cortex, a strip across the top of each hemisphere just behind the motor cortex. Touch is multifaceted in that various sensors in the skin detect it, and it embraces temperature, texture, vibrations and much more. Unsurprisingly, the fingers are the main agents for touch in the body.

4. Parietal lobes

These lobes deal with the sensations of touch, pain and temperature and they contain the sensory cortex. They play a part in spatial orientation, speech and visual perception.

Figure 2.4

5. Angular gyrus

This is a region of the parietal lobe and it is involved in a number of processes related to language and cognition. V.S. Ramachandran, much admired neuroscientist and past deliverer of the Reith lectures, directed a study that showed that the angular gyrus is at least partially responsible for understanding metaphors. Right-handed patients who had damage to their left angular gyrus, and whose speaking and comprehending of English were seemingly unaffected, could not grasp the dual nature of metaphor.

6. Wernicke's area

This region forms part of the cortex on the left posterior section of the left hemisphere. It is named after Karl Wernicke, a German neurologist and psychiatrist, who in 1874 discovered that damage to this area could cause a type of aphasia, which is a loss of ability to produce and/or comprehend language. Damage to this area can result in a speech form that has a natural sounding rhythm and a relatively normal syntax, but otherwise has no recognisable meaning. Wernicke's work initiated the study of this brain area and its role in the understanding and comprehension of spoken language.

7. Occipital lobes

These lobes form one of the most important and one of the largest regions of the brain as they process visual stimuli. They are more simply known as the visual cortex. Located at the back of the head, they form sight centres that decode and analyse incoming signals. As Susan Greenfield notes:

> More is known about how the brain processes nerve signals from the eyes than those from any other sense. (Greenfield, 1996)

The incoming signals make sense only when compared with previously stored cognitive associations. What we attend to then is the co-ordinated functioning of several brain systems. Pat Wolfe, an expert teacher as well as an expert brain writer, notes that visual processing is enhanced when teachers tell their students the objective or purposes for an activity (Wolfe, 2001).

8. The cerebellum

The cerebellum (or 'little brain') makes up about one tenth of the volume of the human brain and it serves to assist balance, body posture and the co-ordination of muscle function. Consider the co-ordination and other skills needed for catching a ball. The timing, the anticipation, the observation of speed and the movement required to have both arm and hand in the right place require a great deal of complex brain functioning. The cerebellum receives nerve signals and compares the instructions and results to modify and fine tune the programme of movement.

The cerebellum, like the brain stem, is primitive in evolutionary terms, and it is found above the brain stem. It is a two-lobed, deeply-folded structure just under the occipital lobes. By the age of two, it has almost reached adult size. In early life the cerebellum stores the patterns of movements for grasping and walking in neural networks that are used for the rest of one's life.

Only recently has the role of the cerebellum in other socially-based functions been recognised; for example, in delaying or accelerating associations and the attentional states that are so important for social exchange. As Ratey points out:

> When it comes to social competence, the inability to shift attention can have devastating consequences. (Ratey, 2001)

He goes on to explain that this inability is one of the features of possible autism, where a baby does not look at something his mother is looking at.

Finally, it is the cerebellum we have to thank for memorising skills like playing a musical instrument or driving a car where we are no longer conscious of precisely what is involved. The cerebellum remembers these processes for us.

9. Spinal cord – the superhighway

The spinal cord is effectively an extension of the brain reaching the rest of the body from a downward facing hole in the base of the skull. A long tube called the vertebral canal protects and encloses the cord. It extends down the spine to the vertebra just above the waist and it is surrounded by membranes and fluid. The cord conveys nerve signals between the brain and the chest and limbs, which are then taken to the muscle fibres via motor neurons. In an adult the cord is about 45 centimetres long and slightly thinner than the index finger. When the human embryo is seven weeks old, the appearance of the spinal cord is clearly visible.

10. Temporal lobe

This region is sometimes said to resemble the shape of a boxing glove. The lobes are part of the cerebrum, and they lie at the side of the brain. Several interlinked functions are housed in this region, which copes principally with hearing and language, but is also implicated in memory, especially auditory memory.

11. The auditory receptive area

This is more commonly called the auditory cortex and it is divided into primary and secondary sections. The primary auditory cortex on the side of the brain is the main incoming and processing area for the nerve signals that represent sounds. The secondary auditory cortex has links with the primary section and other parts of the brain. It helps to co-ordinate hearing with memories, awareness and the other senses. In both auditory areas, the arrangement of neurons is tonotopic:

> this means the sounds of different frequencies stimulate neurons in different arrays ie, rows or columns. (Greenfield, 1996)

The arrangement is such that the neurons at the front, towards the face, respond to high-pitched sounds, and those at the rear to the lower-pitched sounds.

12. Olfactory bulb

Our sense of smell is different from the other senses in that it is hard-wired and connected with memory and emotion. Starting from the first whiff, an odour passes along many pathways through the olfactory system before it is identified. The direct routes to primitive areas mean that certain smells have powerful effects on memories and emotions, and the chances are that we are more influenced by our sense of smell than we think. It seems that smell is based on pattern recognition where an odour activates most of the olfactory cells, and so the identity of the smell lies in the overall pattern of activation.

13. Broca's area

Until the advent of modern imaging techniques, as described in the previous chapter, researchers generally had to wait for autopsy results to make connections between particular behaviour and brain regions. However, in 1861 a Parisian doctor, Paul Broca, provided an important insight when he described a patient who had damage to a small region of the left side of the motor cortex. The area is now known as Broca's area, and the damage here caused the patient to lose the power of speech. People suffering from damage to this area may show a condition known as Broca's aphasia which causes them to have difficulty creating grammatically complex sentences. Their speech is often described as telegraphic because it contains content words alone without the grammar to make sense of them. This is in contrast with Wernicke's aphasia which manifests as a pronounced impairment in comprehension.

A medial view of the brain (Figure 2.5 below)

In this view, we can see four more important parts of the brain.

Brain stem

The autonomic nervous system (ANS) regulates the body's automatic functions of which we are largely unaware. The vital life-maintaining forces of the heartbeat, blood pressure, digestion and breathing are based in the brain stem, which is, as its name implies, the lower part of the brain. Here, the activities are mainly at an unconscious level. The brain stem has three principle functions. The first is its role in conduit functions – all information relayed from the body to the cerebrum and cerebellum and vice versa must pass through the brain

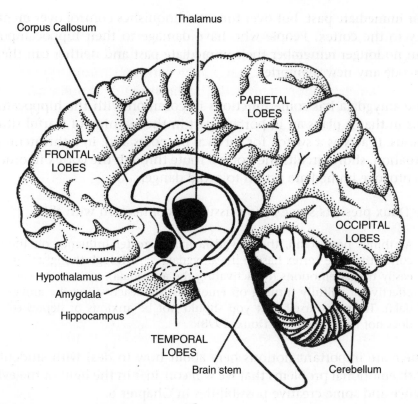

Corpus Callosum

Thalamus

PARIETAL
LOBES

FRONTAL
LOBES

OCCIPITAL
LOBES

Hypothalamus

Amygdala

Hippocampus

TEMPORAL
LOBES

Brain stem

Cerebellum

Figure 2.5   A medial view of the brain

stem. Second, the cranial nerves emerge from the brain stem. Finally, the stem has integrative functions to do with the cardio-vascular system, pain sensitivity, respiratory control and more. Damage to the brain stem is therefore a very serious and life-threatening problem.

Many of the brain stem areas have connections with the hypothalamus, which is the main mediator between the unconscious control systems in the brain stem and the higher mental activities in the cerebrum and cerebral cortex. So if any important signal is perceived, signals from the hypothalamus make the brain stem generate the appropriate response.

The two other areas of note are the hippocampus and the amygdala. Both are relatively small but crucial in terms of their function. The hippocampus derives its name from the Latin for 'seahorse', as it slightly resembles the shape of that creature. It is essential for memory, and also has a role in emotional behaviour, learning and motivation. The hippocampus is also crucial for remembering events in our immediate past, but over time it relinquishes control over memory to the cortex. People who have damage to their hippocampus can no longer remember their immediate past and neither can they encode any new memories.

The amygdala has some functions in common with the hippocampus in that it plays an important part in the learning of fearful situations. It acts as a switch for survival purposes and, in a threatening situation, short-circuits the normal route through the cortex in order to provoke immediate action to avoid danger.

Le Doux presents some serious issues in connection with this:

> As things now stand, the amygdala has a greater influence on the cortex than the cortex has on the amygdala ... Although thoughts can easily trigger emotions (by activating the amygdala), we are not very effective at wilfully turning off emotions (by deactivating the amygdala). Telling yourself that you should not be anxious or depressed does not help much. (Le Doux, 1998)

There are important notions here about how to deal with students with emotional problems that we will consider in the light of the evidence and some creative possibilities in Chapter 6.

Some other terms used in relation to the brain

Triune brain and limbic system
The term 'limbic system' was introduced by Paul Maclean, a physician and noted writer about the brain. He used this term in 1952 to describe the affective regions of the brain. It is still used as a descriptive term, though it is less frequently used by neuroscientists.

Later, in 1970, the term 'Triune brain' was created by MacLean to provide a description of the evolution of the brain in three parts. The reptilian or primitive brain was seen as the first stage of development, followed by the mammalian brain, and finally the last to develop, the neo-cortex. Joseph Le Doux in his writing about 'The Emotional Brain' puts these definitions into context:

> The limbic system was a theory of localization. It proposed to tell us where the emotions reside in the brain. But Maclean and later enthusiasts of the limbic system have not managed to give us a good way of identifying what parts of the brain actually make up the limbic system. (Le Doux, 1998)

The neo-cortex

This term is Latin for 'new bark', and it describes the top layer of the cerebral hemisphere. It is 2–4 millimetres thick and is made up of six layers. It is involved in higher functions such as sensory perception, spatial reasoning and conscious thought. Myelin is a wax-like coating that surrounds the axons of many neurons to ensure that the tiny electrical signals transmitted from the nerve cell and along the axon reach their intended targets.

If you are interested in finding out more about the brain and its structure, you will find the following books particularly helpful.

The Human Mind Explained – Greenfield (1996)

This book which is written by our best known neuroscientist is a beautifully illustrated introduction to the brain and the mind. It is a valuable resource for students of all ages in both primary and secondary school.

A User's Guide to the Brain – Ratey (2001)

John Ratey is a professor of psychiatry at Harvard who has produced a highly readable reference book. He sets out to show how the structure and chemistry of the brain shape our perceptions, emotions and behaviour and how flexible and adaptable the brain is to new demands and conditions.

The Learning Brain – Blakemore and Frith (2005)

The authors work at the Institute of Cognitive Neuroscience in London and they have produced an authoritative description of lessons learned from neuroscience that have relevance for education. They explode myths about the brain; for example the notion that we use only 10 per cent of the brain, and they are cautious in applying findings from neuroscience to the classroom. This is a valuable book for teachers.

3

Pay attention and get connected!

In the five sections of this chapter we consider different aspects of attention, and examine evidence from research in this fast-growing field of study. Here you will learn more about:

- why attention is essential for intellectual development and how it causes the brain to create connections;

- barriers to attention in a technological age, and the problems for some children with watching television;

- the importance for children of being physically active to develop their brains and evidence of the impact of technology on children's performance;

- the discovery of mirror neurons and the importance of first-hand experiences for sensory, and therefore brain, development;

- moving to school, drawing on evidence about attention that affects how children join school and make progress.

The chapter ends with a consideration of attention as the new formal discipline underpinning learning through the pioneering work of the neuroscientists Posner and Rothbart.

No attention – no learning!

The notion of paying attention has always been seen as important by teachers. Now neuroscientists are beginning to explain why it is so vital for learners. As long ago as the end of the nineteenth century, the psychologist William James identified two key processes involved with attention – volition and inhibition. By these terms he meant both the desire and curiosity to focus, and the ability to screen out other stimuli.

More than fifty years later Donald Hebb, a 'visionary psychologist', asserted that:

> Neurons that fire together wire together. (Hebb, 1949)

This idea, explained in the previous chapter, amplifies James's explanation by showing how patterns of neurons develop from attention and become stronger with use.

Attention creates connections

Neuroscientists have developed detailed and complex theories of how the brain creates neural connections during the course of attending. Susan Greenfield provides a simple explanation:

- incoming cell X is active;

- it excites a target cell Y;

- the synapse between X and Y is strengthened and becomes more effective in chemical signalling (Greenfield, 1997).

This basic process underpins the brain's plasticity for learning. As part of their explanation of 'Neural Darwinism', Edelman expresses the same ideas in a way that accounts for individual differences:

> during development, neurons extend myriads of branching processes in many directions. This branching generates extensive variability in the connection patterns of that individual and creates an immense and diverse repertoire of neural circuits. Then, neurons strengthen and weaken their connections according to their individual patterns of electrical activity: Neurons that fire together wire together. As a result, neurons in a group are more closely connected to each other than to neurons in other groups. (Edelman, 2000)

Essentially this means that some synapses are strengthened through firing and some are weakened through lack of use, and that this is to the individual. Edelmann stresses repeatedly that one of the iking features of each brain is its individuality and variability.

Focusing attention

William James was the first person to explain that the very act of attending to something keeps it in the conscious mind for longer. He uses the term 'Effortful attention' to describe the process which stops ideas fading. Schwartz and Begley (2002) develop this notion in their research illustrating how the mind shapes the brain:

> We go through our lives seeing countless objects that we do not pay attention to. Without attention, the image (or the sound or the feel – attention plays a role in every sense) does not register in the mind and may not be stored even briefly in the memory.

This raises the question of what happens when the brain does attend to a stimulus. Schwartz and Begley's explanation is extremely important for our understanding of learning:

> Selectively focusing attention on target images significantly enhances neuronal responses to them … selective attention can strengthen or weaken neural processing in the visual cortex.

So paying attention, an activity usually regarded as an attribute of the mind, actually determines the structure of the brain. Focused attention strengthens the channels for processing information and so leads to better learning. The processes involved with attention are therefore fundamental to our understanding of what learning is about, and to a large extent it is true that in particular ways we can become what we give attention to. Children who are taught and encouraged to attend have advantages over those who are not.

∿ Point for reflection

When you have a spare moment glance around you and just notice four or more different features of your environment. Don't think about them, just note them. Next, spend 30 seconds focusing on one of your thumbs and notice all the distinguishing features in as much detail as you can. Finally, notice the difference between the two experiences and how the second one really engages the brain to make distinctions and creates the initial connections to record and return to.

Consciousness and attention

Some neuroscientists approach attention through theories of consciousness. Antonio Damasio is one of these and he sees consciousness as 'the last mystery in the elucidation of the mind', and as the means to 'a life examined for better or worse'. He is clear that consciousness can be separated from low level attention (Damasio, 1999). The writer John Ratey explains:

> Consciousness and attention are the foundations on which we create an understanding of the world. Together they form the ground upon which we build a sense of who we are, as we define ourselves in relation to the myriad physical and social worlds we inhabit. They also are the basic functions that give rise to the mind. (Ratey, 2001)

He explains that the input-output model of the brain that was dominant in the last century has been superseded by recent research showing how neurons are actively engaged in choosing whether and how to respond to stimuli. He describes a four step model of the attention system.

1   At the lowest level of monitoring, the brain stem maintains our vigilance, or general degree of arousal.

2   At the next level, the brain's motor centre allows us to physically reorient our bodies and redirect our senses to the next threat or to food.

3   The limbic system accomplishes both the detection and reward of novelty.

4   Finally the cortex, and especially the frontal lobes, integrate attention with our short- and long-term goals.

These levels of attention suggest both the complexity and importance of the process of attending. They reflect an underpinning theme of this book, which is that attention and survival are clearly connected.

Attention and survival

Attention has evolved as a crucial part of our survival apparatus, a vital survival skill. Unsurprisingly, in terms of the contemporary view of the brain as being an interdependent and integrated system, Ratey argues that the attention systems are widely spread throughout the brain. The frontal lobes, limbic system, brain stem, sense organs and hippocampus are all involved. The gatekeeper is the hippocampus which plays a vital role in long-term memory. (See the work of Maguire et al. (1997) with taxi drivers, and the expansion of the hippocampus to store 'the knowledge'.)

Novelty and reward are two of the main forces that direct our attention. Excessive response to novelty can be seen in children with Attention Deficit Hyperactivity Disorder (ADHD). They are frequently distracted by new events around them which they find more rewarding than sustained focus on a single activity. Ratey suggests that ADHD can be thought of at one level as an addiction to the present, and relates the behaviour to studies of monkeys who are also unable to sustain attention. He notes that the monkeys will prioritise tasks according to which offers the most immediate gratification, and that this impulsive behaviour limits their ability to maintain long-term survival goals (Ratey, 2001).

The structure of the attention process

The second of the key attention processes identified by James is inhibition. The brain has the ability to suppress activity in other senses when attention is focused and sustained. Robinson cites an example from research in which participants' brains were scanned during an experiment where they were expecting a touch on the arm, but didn't receive it. The scan showed that attention was focused on the arm, and reduced towards other parts of the body where touch was not expected. He argues that attention sculpts the brain by increasing the rate at which particular sets of synapses fire – that is, when a neuron fires a signal which is received by another cell (Robertson 1999).

James also discusses the importance of sustaining attention. He describes 'monotony override', a mechanism that enables us to keep attending to repetitive, but necessary, activities where there is no new input or other 'reward'. A modern day example of this would be the kind of attention needed when driving on a long journey, where there are periods with little change in experience, and where switching off attention altogether could have disastrous consequences!

Rita Carter divides the process of attention into three separate functions: arousal, orientation and focus. Arousal is the first level of interest or curiosity, orientation is adjusting the head and body to attend, and focus is the sustaining of attention. She notes the areas of the brain that are particularly active with each function. The first element, arousal, is mainly controlled by the reticular activating system which lies at the top of the brain stem. It contains neurons that affect consciousness, the sleep/wake cycle and the level of activity in the brain. Orientation is connected with the superior colliculus which turns the eyes to the new stimulus. At the same time, the parietal cortex disengages attention from the current object of attention. Finally the lateral pulvinar above the brain stem locks on to the stimulus to maintain attention (Carter, 1998).

Attention and evolution

At a more primal level, attention is vitally important for survival. Edelman clearly relates the selectivity aspect of attention to the processes of evolution and survival.

> An animal that is hungry or being threatened has to select an object or an action from many possible ones. Possessing such ability makes it possible to achieve a goal that would otherwise be interfered with by the attempt to undertake two incompatible actions simultaneously. Survival may depend critically on this ability. (Edelman, 2000)

Edelman also notes how fragile this function is and therefore how important it is to cultivate it.

Another important part of the brain that is crucial for survival is the amygdala. Joseph Le Doux, in his pioneering work on the emotions, discovered the significance of this almond-shaped region that can bypass the normal processes of the brain in response to fear. He illustrates how this occurs by means of a story:

> Imagine walking in the woods. A crackling sound occurs. It goes straight to the amygdala through the thalamic pathway. The sound also goes from the thalamus to the cortex, which recognizes the sound to be of a dry twig that snapped under the weight of your boot, or that of a rattlesnake shaking its tail. But by the time the cortex has figured this out, the amygdala is already starting to defend against the snake. (Le Doux, 1998)

In a more recent work, Le Doux also explains how:

> Emotional arousal has powerful influences over cognitive processing, including attention, perception, memory and decision making. (Le Doux, 2002)

This statement indicates just how important the emotions are for learning in the classroom and, as we shall see in Chapter 4, they are closely connected with attention.

So far we have seen that:

- attention is vital both for learning and survival;

- the focusing of attention can both create and strengthen neural networks;

- attention involves a set of processes which include arousal, inhibition, orientation, volition, and action in accordance with goals;

- interest, curiosity and enthusiasm are predispositions for attention;

- attending is a positive and active process, rather than a passive state;

- without attention, little of consequence may be stored in the brain.

These factors are all significant in the attention process and as we shall see are also vital elements in the development of learning.

 Point for reflection

The key question here is: how we can nurture the skills of attention both at home and at school as the basis for further learning? The section about the importance of guided experience later in this chapter provides some suggestions.

Attention as a starting point

My interest in attention was stimulated by a chance meeting. Some years ago my wife and I were walking the Pennine Way and we met a number of interesting people, one of whom was a physicist, and quite eminent in his field. While sharing the walk, I asked him if there was a particular point in his childhood when he had decided to take up physics. He thought for a while and said that all that came into his mind was an experience when he was ten years old. At this time in his primary school, he had the opportunity to observe a moth's wing in a binocular microscope. In gazing at the wing, he was moved by the sheer beauty of the delicate patterns and the symmetry and he became deeply immersed in the experience. He felt that this was the point that led him into studying biology and in time also to studying physics. The simple act of attending to something of interest can have long-lasting effects.

Attention then is not merely something that teachers expect their pupils to 'pay', but a survival-based and essential foundation for intellectual development. It is not just coincidence that some of the most important inventions and scientific breakthroughs have occurred following quite simple acts of attention and observation, evidently a vital part of scientific method.

Now it is time to consider some of the obstacles and challenges that make the apparently simple act of attending rather more difficult for some children than it should be.

Problems for today's children concerning attention – the message that we don't want to hear!

The themes in this section show that although television and other technologies are of huge benefit to children for both entertainment and education, there are downsides. These include the impact of technology on literacy, and the need on occasions for pupils to give undivided attention to their work rather than multi-tasking. We also consider the importance of sleep and the work of Dr Aric Sigman concerning the negative impact of television on children's performance and wellbeing.

Environmental factors and attention

Studies of what prevents children from paying attention in the postmodern world began in the 1990s in the USA, and in particular with the work of Jane Healey, an educational psychologist. Her first work, *Endangered Minds* (1990), was an assault on the negative aspects of the increased tempo of contemporary life, including the use of television, videos and computer games. She suggested in this work that children who were surrounded by such fast-paced visual stimuli were not prepared for academic learning, where the emphasis was on face-to-face interaction, interactive language, reflective problem-solving, creative play and sustained attention. Controversially, she claimed that children's brains were being changed by contemporary culture. The same plasticity mentioned previously (and which is a main focus in Chapter 6) works to contract rather than expand the abilities of the brain. Her evidence for this assertion was a steep decline in the amounts of time that children were reading and talking. She argued:

> The state of literacy in the United States today is declining so precipitously, while video and computer technologies are becoming so powerful, that the act of reading may well be on the way to obsolescence. (Healy, 1990)

One of the main arguments that Healey pursues is that attention is reduced in many children through environmental factors. This is not a Luddite rant against the modern world, but a thoughtful critique informed by a perspective based on an understanding of brain function. She cites the difficulty that some children have in screening out unwanted stimuli. Young children, she says, are notoriously 'stimulus-bound', and thus they tend to be highly distractible. She reasons that adults – who help children to use their pre-frontal cortex by putting thought and action ahead of instant gratification – are helping children to sustain attention. Moreover, she suggests that 'shovelling information' into young children will serve little purpose unless children learn to use their brains to reflect on meaning, plan ahead and follow through constructively. She laments the fact that standard IQ tests in the USA do not measure these higher-order skills.

The detrimental environmental factors Healy points to are:

- toxic substances and foods that may predispose children to attention problems;

- noisy environments that cause children to tune out rather than tune in;

- sedentary lifestyles;

- failure by adults to act as constructive, thoughtful coaches for children.

A problem with Healy's work is that while there is a lot of supporting anecdotal evidence, only a relatively small amount of research evidence was available at the time of her writing. However, the factors she identified are similar to those explored by Sue Palmer in *Toxic Childhood* (2006), a major contemporary work from the UK, and published some sixteen years later with the benefit of recent research findings.

Palmer identifies three key principles for learning that children must grasp and which have been at the heart of civilisation throughout human history. The first of these, and by implication the most important, is the ability to maintain attention 'even when something doesn't particularly interest them'. She adds the rider that 'if you can't attend – or if you're only prepared to attend to things that interest you', then school is going to be problematic (Palmer, 2006). Her analysis is that time is needed for attention; it cannot be learned at 'electric speed'. This is a vital factor that we will return to later in this chapter, as pupils also show concern at the lack of time to complete work.

 Point for reflection

Reading is a particular use of attention that requires support to sustain it. How then can technology in the home be used to give children support and sustenance for reading?

The limitations of multi-tasking

The neurologist Dr Richard Restak covers the themes of brain plasticity and attention in his book *The New Brain* (2003) which considers the impact of contemporary life on the brain. From the outset, he describes intelligence as partly genetic and partly environmental and therefore modifiable. In other words, intelligence is not a fixed entity:

> Moreover, thanks to our own efforts we can modify our brain's structure and improve aspects of our intelligence, even if we don't raise our overall I.Q. on standard tests. (Restak, 2003)

He argues further that brain plasticity not only responds to the training and influences that we choose, but also for good or bad to the technology that surrounds us. Television, movies, cell phones, e-mail, video games and the internet all have an impact. He describes the blistering pace of modern life and the demands to improve our performance year after year.

In reviewing the evidence to show that the current technologies are forcing our brains to restructure themselves and accommodate to a world of multiple identity and presence, he calls into question the notion of 'multi-tasking' which may have particular resonance for learning. He challenges the reification of multi-tasking and cites various research studies which show that it is not as efficient as most of us have been led to believe. He explains that whenever we try to do two things at once, our attention is actually directed to one or other activity rather than to both at once. In addition, the shift from one activity to another can take up to seven-tenths of a second. In an experiment to investigate multi-tasking, subjects were asked to perform various tasks while reading; the efficiency of readers who were mentally rotating objects at the same time decreased by 53 per cent. A similar reduction occurred with young adults who rapidly switched between working out arithmetical problems and practical tasks. The research showed that not only speed of performance but also accuracy suffered. Restak concludes:

> In short, the brain is designed to work most efficiently when it works on a single task and for sustained rather than intermittent and alternating periods of time. (Restak, 2003)

Another enquiry which supports the view that multi-tasking is not helpful to learning is that by Rubenstein (2001). In a study sponsored by the US Federal Aviation Administration and the University of Michigan, four groups of young adults switched between tasks involving mathematical problems, or identifying geometric shapes. The researchers found that, for all types of tasks, participants lost time when they switched back and forth. They drew upon previous research to propose a model of brain activity in multi-tasking: the brain has to manage goal shifting (choosing to switch to a new task), followed by switching off the cognitive rules of the old task and switching on the rules for the new task. The study concluded that multi-tasking is not normally very efficient (Rubenstein, 2001).

So, although we can train our brains to multi-task, it is essential to realise that our overall performance on each of the tasks is going to be less efficient than if we performed one thing at one time. This is a valuable insight for students of all ages where learning and doing one thing at a time needs to be the maxim.

Learning and undivided attention

A study by the National Academy of Sciences in the United States reached a similar conclusion. The researchers contrasted single and dual task learning. They explained that with single task learning the temporal lobe is used for declarative learning: a student will recall what has been learned and the context for later recall. However, with dual task learning brain processes compete with each other and the brain defaults to habit learning and does not recall purpose or context easily. In the conclusion they comment:

> One thing at a time is faded advice, heretical in a culture that prides itself on juggling outrageous numbers of duties. The human brain doesn't change at the whim of the human schedule, and children still learn best when they learn in a calm, orderly manner. (Sciences, 2006)

More support for this view comes from studies at the Kaiser Family Foundation, based in California. They found that children spend a steady 6.5 hours a day using electronic media, but pack 8.5 hours of media exposure into that time, through multi-tasking with different technologies. They also discovered that children tackling homework while sending messages via the internet end up spending 50 per cent longer than if they had done each task separately. Professor Stephen Monsell of Exeter University questioned how well children can study with multimedia and multi-tasking:

> If you want to think profoundly about one thing, you have to concentrate for a long time. If you are answering your mobile phone every five minutes, it is less likely a thoughtful and coherent piece of work will emerge. (Cited in Elliott, 2006)

There are of course exceptions to this rule. It does seem, for instance, that the brain can cope with doodling while carrying out a telephone call. The novelist Ian McEwan reminded us in his (2006) novel *Saturday* than multi-tasking can help some people to perform better. The central character, a neurosurgeon, remarks that 'listening to music can enhance efficiency amongst those who work with their hands'. Similarly, the work of John MacBeath has shown that some students are happier and more effective in doing their homework in a naturalistic setting at home with background music rather than in isolation (MacBeath, 1997).

〰 **Point for reflection**

> Multi-tasking, or managing several activities at the same time, is now a normal part of daily life. How can we balance advice and practice in schools with an awareness that, for accuracy, our brains respond best with one function at a time? Part of the answer to this question is to ensure that pupils understand more about their brains and therefore how best to use them.

Some consequences for children of television watching

One of the most challenging and sensitive problems with attention concerns our patterns of television viewing. It is challenging in that some of the evidence suggests that serious problems may arise for those children who watch too much television, and it is sensitive because many parents will react in a personal way to any criticism of their family viewing habits. Neuroscientist Ian Robertson, for example, presents his views in a forthright way:

> Watching television is a case of your attention being passively massaged by the sounds, stories and colours on the screen. Without attention to what we are doing, our brain will not be sculpted to anything like the same degree that it will if we give our full attention to what is happening. Parents are the main sculptors of their children's brains. Just as sculpting the brain requires effort, attention and practice by the child, so it needs the same things from busy parents who have their own worries and preoccupations. (Robertson, 1999)

The quality of attention, or lack of it, is one of the crucial concerns about television watching for children, but it is not the only one. The work of Aric Sigman is a major assault on the nation's favourite pastime. Where children are concerned, he argues that television watching:

- stunts the development of children's brains;

- may permanently hinder children's educational progress;

- increases the likelihood of children developing ADHD;

- is a major cause of depression. (Sigman, 2005)

How television watching dominates children's lives

Professor Sigman expresses concerns about the amount of time spent watching television. The average American watches four hours per day, and children, he says, now spend more time watching a television screen than they spend in school. An average 6-year-old will have watched TV for nearly one full year of their life and may well have had more eye contact with television characters than with their parents. Sigman's most serious claim is that watching television during the first few years of life distorts the wiring of a child's brain. He also cites evidence from a study from Oxford University which showed that children who have televisions in their bedrooms are being deprived of up to a month of sleep in a year, adversely affecting their performance in school (Sigman, 2005).

Marian Diamond cites Patricia Greenfield, an expert on how television affects a child's development, who shows similar concerns. She writes that by the age of 18-years-old the average American child will have spent more of his or her life watching television than in any other single activity but sleep (Diamond, 1998). Greenfield also notes that in inner city areas families often use the television as a constant backdrop to other activities. Sigman quotes similar figures and notes that we average one full day of watching television per week. 'Television has become not just our favourite pastime: it is our prime time, our main source of common experience'. This is also acknowledged by Ofsted. In May 2006, the then Chief Inspector of schools said that 'Parents must make sure their children do not stay up late watching television' (press release, 19 May 2006). This statement was in the context of advice to parents concerning the 'serious responsibility' of preparing children for going to school and working hard. The more 'serious responsibility' though, may be to understand the implications of our use of technology.

> Ironically, the more technology has allowed us to talk to each other, the less we seem to talk to our children. (Palmer, 2006)

Television watching and sleep

Television watching can generate a downward spiral and create a second strand of concern in terms of the impact of television watching on health. Sigman cites Belgian research showing that children with televisions in their bedroom go to bed 'significantly later' and become much more tired. The Oxford study previously mentioned also showed that such children were often irritable and drowsy next day, the opposite in fact of being in an optimal state of readiness for learning (Wiggs, 2004).

Evidence shows that children who sleep poorly are more than twice as likely to end up smoking, drinking and using drugs at ages twelve and fourteen (Wong, 2004). A good night's sleep is also the foundation for good health, with a positive impact upon the immune system and the production of melatonin, a hormone that promotes sleep.

Another strand of argument that Sigman uses concerns attention as a condition for being alive. He suggests that damage to attention compromises our ability to live and experience as fully as we might. He claims also that attention has become a commodity that is the subject of competition in a capitalist society. Children in particular are vulnerable to the forces of competition as potential consumers where they are carefully targeted by particular brand advertising.

Attentional inertia

Central to concern over television watching and attention is the notion of the inertia which takes place after a short period of viewing. Sigman describes the process:

> Most of our stares at television are brief, lasting less than three seconds and highly prone to termination. However, if we continue to stare at the screen, then after about fifteen seconds 'attentional inertia' takes over. This inertia is absolutely vital for learning as it helps a child to keep attending to events, even when it is difficult. (Sigman, 2005)

He cites researchers who claim that children's programmes corrupt a child's attention because they demand constant attentional shifts by their viewers, but do not require them to pay prolonged attention to given events. It seems that the much admired author Norman Mailer had also spotted the problems for television and attention. He was asked what he would change in American society for the better, and he replied that 'with the advent of television the nature of concentration was altered', and that narratives were truncated because of commercial breaks. The power of narrative is hugely important in this context. It is the locus for sustained attention and a recurring theme in examining brain damage and healing through brain imaging (Xu et al., 2005). Mailer subsequently concluded that television commercials had to go (Mailer, 2005).

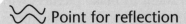 Point for reflection

The issues of sleep and television watching are highly sensitive as they involve our individual rights to make appropriate choices. The evidence suggests though that each is important for pupils' learning and that both need careful consideration. In order to help pupils to achieve their best in school, a form of discussion between parents and teachers is needed, leading to a written 'accord' stating the agreed best practice. What would best suit your setting as a form of working agreement and how might it be achieved?

Television and social behaviour – the issue of trance!

A further strand of Sigman's work considers the impact of television watching on brain function. He compares and contrasts the effects of watching television and hypnosis. He notes that the two activities have similar effects in that they tune out the left hemisphere. Both can lead to the danger of falling into a trance-like state, leaving the right brain – which processes information emotionally and uncritically – unimpeded. Although this may be desirable in hypnosis, Sigman argues that there is a resulting impact on our use of free will, as our capacity for controlling our actions may become distorted. Most worrying of all he says, is the possible effect on the development of the frontal lobes. This region, as we saw earlier, plays an important role in decision-making and is sometimes called the executive area of the brain. A report from the World Federation of Neurology expressed concern over the way that visual electronic media are halting the process of frontal lobe development, and affecting children's ability to control potentially antisocial elements of their behaviour (Kawashima, 2001). To mitigate the effects, the article suggests that children should be encouraged to play outside with other children, to interact and communicate as much as possible. This argument overlaps with suggestions about childhood from several writers, including those from Sue Palmer in *Toxic Childhood*. (2006)

To counteract the negative aspects of television, Dr Sigman recommends the following for children;

- being physically active and reading rather than watching television;

- engaging with activities that require them to make pictures with their imagination; for example by listening to or telling stories, including audio books, painting, playing and reading;

- fostering children's innate ability to entertain themselves and to play with others.

The Green remedy

Dr Sigman also has a further recommendation – going Green! Plants, he explains, have many beneficial effects, and exposure to greenery counters much of the stress of contemporary living. He notes many research studies to support this hypothesis, including one scientist from the University of Reading who suggests that:

> a human being needs some exposure to plants or other green space for at least a couple of hours each week. (Sigman, 2005)

This could be very important for children, especially those living in an inner-city environment. The explanation for this:

> seems to revolve around the way greenery effortlessly engages our attention, allowing us to attend without paying attention. (Sigman, 2005)

He also believes that there is an 'attentional restoration theory', whereby certain activities cause a temporary 'attention fatigue' which is corrected when our underlying attention system has an opportunity to rest. A natural setting may recharge our attention system.

Leisure activities and attention

Marian Diamond is one of the world's leading neuroscientists and she is well known for her extensive research into the effects of enrichment on the brain. She too expresses concern over the impact of television, and describes how TV and video games induce forms of 'intellectual entropy', where the brain sinks to its lowest level of energy use and lowest mental output. She begins from the standpoint of the brain as a highly plastic organ:

> The emerging message is clear. The brain with its complex architecture and limitless potential, is a highly plastic, constantly changing entity that is powerfully shaped by our experiences in childhood and throughout life. (Diamond, 1998)

One of her concerns with attention is that all children should have rich opportunities outside school to challenge and extend their intellectual growth. She instances the work of the researcher Reed Larson, whose work aims to support children in moving from impulsivity and distractibility to voluntary attention. Larson's team analysed children's leisure activities in terms of the levels of motivation and attention they generated. They found activities could be classified by:

- high intrinsic motivation and low attention (for example, a form of play that a child enjoys, but with little challenge);

- high attention and low intrinsic motivation (for example, a task where the pupil wants to please the teacher but finds the task uninteresting);

- high intrinsic motivation and high attention (a state close to that of flow, or 'self absorbed enjoyment', as defined by the psychologist Csikszentmihalyi (2002)).

- low attention and low intrinsic motivation (a state of boredom due to an uninteresting and unchallenging task).

Having studied these motivational and attentional states and the processes of moving towards the preferred zones, Larson claims that leisure activities such as cooking, building models, solving puzzles, playing basketball, or learning the flute all contribute to children achieving satisfaction and forgetting their problems. He explains:

> While wrapped up in a favourite pastime with a high concentration of attention, children experience positive emotions that can't be achieved in any other way quite as successfully. (cited in Diamond, 1998)

In a resource guide, Diamond recommends a wide range of age-related leisure activities that includes books, hobbies, CDs, sports equipment and musical instruments. She also commends the practice of television-free periods for children as a means of widening their horizons to discover other and more challenging possibilities for leisure.

 Point for reflection

Evidence points to the value of leisure activities as an essential part of children's brain growth and development. While the pressures of accountability in school are so great, it may be that parents, in conjunction with teachers, can lead many of the activities that are badly needed.

The effect of television on attainment

Diamond's inspiration for television-free periods for children was taken from a major critique of the impact of television viewing on the behaviour, attitudes and attainment of children by Marie Winn (2002). Much of the evidence for her study was derived from anecdotes. Many of these are quite telling; for example, the views of the director of a Harlem centre for deprived pre-school children who explains that child after child arrives at the school virtually mute, 'unable to speak a single sentence'. This, he says, is usually diagnosed as a speech problem:

> but most often I have found it to be simply the result of hearing bad English, listening to nothing but television and being spoken to hardly at all. (Winn, 2002)

Winn describes this and other problems as the difficulty of attending and interacting because television takes away so many possibilities and leaves children more passive.

The National Assessment of Educational Progress USA found that there was a steady decline in academic skills at all grade levels during the 1970s and 1980s. There was one skill in particular that showed a significant decline, and this was the ability to use inferential comprehension. Winn instances the work of Howard Gardner, who in Project Zero set up an experiment where one set of pupils had a story read to them, and the other set watched and listened to the story as a television presentation. The results, she says, were startling:

Compared to the children who saw the presentation on television, the book version children remembered more of the story when tested at the end of their session and were able to recall more details when asked to do so on their own. In addition, the book children were far more likely to repeat the exact words or phrases that had appeared in the book, while the video children were inclined to paraphrase. (cited in Winn, 2002)

In contrasting the experiences, Gardner concluded that television emerges as a much more self-contained and limited experience for children with the visual component as paramount, whereas the book experience encourages children to make connections with other realms of life.

These ideas are similarly framed by Postman, an American cultural critic and communications theorist, when he says that:

although language is heard on television, and sometimes assumes importance, it is the picture that dominates the viewers' consciousness and carries the critical meanings. To say it as simply as one can, people watch television, they do not read it. (Postman, 1994)

He contrasts the experience of watching television with reading, by noting how books vary in their lexical and syntactic complexity, while television presents information in a form that is undifferentiated in its accessibility. No child or adult, he claims, becomes better at watching television by doing more of it!

Marie Winn shows the damaging effects of television watching for children, ranging from a decrease in the quality of family life and the rituals of doing things together, to an increase in violence and a lack of civic involvement. However, the theme of attention underpins most of her arguments. She summarises the importance of attention, quoting those neuroscientists mentioned by Blakeslee who suggest that:

among the most important of the environmental factors that might affect neurological development are the language and eye contact that an infant is exposed to. (Blakeslee, 1997)

This contrasts with the nature of attention when children watch television: there are some indications that television viewing creates a trance-like state, which is essentially a non-verbal and passive state:

Normal active cognition is temporarily replaced by a state of mind more akin to meditation. (Winn, 2002)

The influence of computers on attention

Clearly there are serious dangers with television watching, but there are issues about other electronic media as well. In her second book in 1998, *Failing to Connect* Jane Healy considers the use of computers at home and at school. She describs her own journey in educational computing 'from bedazzled advocacy to troubled scepticism'. Her main premise – based on personal experience plus many interviews and observations – is that computers have been accepted in education uncritically, and that their benefits have been oversold. She illustrates the ways in which some computing products emphasise performance goals at the expense of learning, and frequently encourage convergent rather than divergent thinking (Healy, 1998). She argues that, as with television, attention is easily transfixed by content 'unworthy of the attention' that it compels. She disputes some common misapprehensions about the nature of learning and computers, and suggests that:

- using computers will not make your child smarter;

- information is not the be-all and end-all of learning;

- facility with a computer signifies nothing special about a child's intelligence.

She also emphasises the importance of personal interaction in learning:

- simple parent-child activities such as hobbies, games and reading together have a solid research record for improving academic skills;

- the key to the positive use of any medium is the quality of adult-child interaction.

The final point is one that can hardly be made too strongly, and applies equally to teachers and parents. We shall return to it later in the chapter.

The theme of attention is central to Healy's arguments. She chooses three phases of the activities involved in paying attention (similar to those described earlier in this chapter), to illustrate some of the problems she identifies. In the *selection phase* of attention she explains that 'sensory bombardment' can tune out the ability to focus on one particular chosen field. Then she claims that in the subsequent *action and planning phase*, many software programs actually take this responsibility away from the child. In the area of *sustained attention* she argues that it may be the high stimulus value of the program that sustains interest rather than an act of choice. This is the aspect of attention that she finds most worrying.

Strategies for improving attention with the use of computers

In conclusion, Healy suggests six strategies or guidelines for improving attention and supporting children in computer activities.

- Be aware, particularly with young children, of the impact of the software on the senses, such as excessively loud noise or garish colour effects.

- Make sure your child gets sufficient exercise and regular breaks from the computer activity.

- Don't let screen time interfere with bedtime.

- Ensure age-appropriate material, to avoid anxiety or depression.

- Watch your child and see who or what is controlling their responses.

- Encourage your child to discuss the programs, and their strategies and plans.

Computers and creative thinking

Healy distinguishes between learning and performance goals, defining learning goals as improving skills through competing against oneself, and performance goals as improving skills through competing against others. She believes performance goals tend to be convergent, leading to the 'right' answer, while learning goals may be more divergent and conducive to creative thinking. While accepting that both are necessary, she fears that much computer software is more concerned with performance, and therefore of less educational value. She connects this point with the absence of possibilities for metacognition (the processes of thinking used in learning, and the language of reflection).

Healy (1990) suggests a five-point programme to help pupils to deal with attention, which emphasises speech and asking themselves valuable questions.

1 Stop. Think. What is my task? Identify the problem in words.

2 What is my plan? Talk through the possible steps to a solution

3 How should I begin? Analyse the first step.

4 How am I doing? Am I on task?

5 Stop. Look back. How did I do? Analyse the results.

In conclusion, she notes that language is vital to problem-solving and helps to develop the pre-frontal cortex. She is deeply concerned that if language and the ability to mediate problems with words are subordinated to electronic constructs, then they may never be regained.

Attention as a perishable commodity

The arguments that television can have damaging effects on the social and intellectual development of children are substantial and well made, even though precise evidence about the impact on the brain is less developed. What is surprising is how little influence these arguments have upon public practice and media coverage in the UK. This leads the main British academic critic Sigman, a man to whom parents and the education community should be grateful, to conclude:

> The link between watching television and physical and psychological damage is neither a concoction nor an exaggeration. Rather, the reverse. (Sigman, 2005)

The issue of attention is at the heart of his arguments concerning the serious consequences of early television watching:

> Children who watch television between ages one and three have a significantly increased risk of developing attentional problems by the time they are seven. For every hour of television a child watches per day, there is a nine per cent increase in attentional damage. (Sigman, 2005)

As he points out, attention is a perishable commodity, and as such it needs to be maintained by nurturing and sustenance.

The ambivalence over taking action on this evidence is described in a (2004) paper by Jane Healy, where she illustrates the gap between recommendations and actual practice. She writes that guidelines from the American Academy of Pediatrics suggested:

- no screen time for children of 2-years-old;

- no more than one to two hours a day of quality television and video for older children;

- no electronic media in young children's rooms.

The actual picture found in one survey was very different:

- 43 per cent of 2-year-olds watch television every day;

- 68 per cent of 2-year-olds spend over two hours each day using screen media;

- 26 per cent of 2-year-olds have a television in their bedroom.

These data reflect the dilemma for parents. How concerned should they be about the evidence, and how reliable is it anyway? I believe that the evidence cited in this chapter so far is substantial and should be taken very seriously by all those concerned with children's welfare and mental health. Furthermore, an understanding of the impact of television and electronic media should inform the strategies for raising standards in schools, particularly regarding writing at Key Stage 2. Children today spend a great deal of time with visual media, and their experience of writing is often limited to texting and e-mail, so the written form in school is more challenging and seen as less relevant to their lives than it was two generations ago. When the brain is considered from an evolutionary perspective, it can be seen that speaking and listening are survival-based skills and that they build the frameworks on which reading and writing develop. As we shall see later in this chapter, the foundations for learning need to be based on guided experience accompanied by social interaction and spoken language, and the quality of pupils' attention is essential for success.

The evidence then points to a set of overlapping issues that concerns parents even more than teachers – the use of technology in the home, the cultivation of attention, the need for high quality leisure experiences, the management of sleep, and television watching and other related social issues. These are indeed very challenging. There are no easy or elegant solutions as they all impinge on personal values and involve matters of judgement. We may now need to consider the formation at school level of a 'Parent Congress', whose purpose would be to give guidance on the best home-based practices to enable pupils to get the most from their education. This would be purely advisory and quite separate from existing home/school liaison groups. Guidance for parents that included television viewing, sleep, technology in the bedroom and homework would provide valuable starting points for such a group.

 Point for reflection

Is there a forum with parents in your school or setting that exists or could be created to discuss the issues of television viewing, patterns of sleep and the development of attention?

The discovery of mirror neurons: imitation and modelling in learning and development

Now we turn to recent evidence concerning another aspect of attention which is vital for both survival and learning. This is the discovery of mirror neurons and their function in imitation and modelling.

In the year 2000, one of the world's leading neuroscientists made a remarkable statement about a recent discovery in his field:

> The discovery of mirror neurons in the frontal lobes of monkeys, and their potential relevance to human brain evolution, is the single most important unreported or unpublicized story of the decade. I predict that mirror neurons will do for psychology what DNA did for biology: they will provide a unifying framework and help explain a host of mental abilities that have hitherto remained mysterious and inaccessible to experiments. (Ramachandran, 2000)

Ramachandran claims that this discovery represents the fifth revolution (the others include the work of Copernicus, Darwin, and also Watson and Crick with DNA). The discovery he is referring to is the

research by Giacomo Rizzolatti and Vittorio Gallese i
demonstrating that neurons in the pre-motor cortex of a
brain fire or are activated when it observes another monke
object. This discovery and subsequent work suggest that th
are part of a network that enables us to see the world from another
person's point of view, hence the term 'mirror neuron'. In a more
recent paper, he cites research from the USA which found that cells
in the anterior cingulate which normally fire when you prick a
patient with a needle will also fire when a patient watches another
patient experiencing the same event (Iacoboni et al., 2005).

Ramachandran refers to his own work using electro-encephalograph
recordings, which show that autistic children appear to lack mirror
neurons. This discovery may help to explain the defining characteristics of autism – a lack of empathy and a theory of other minds
(Ramachandran, 2006). This study of mirror neurons is an emerging
field of inquiry embracing the disciplines of developmental psychology, evolutionary biology, neuroscience, language evolution and
experimental psychology. Although it is in its infancy, there are several possible areas of development here with implications for learning and teaching. These could include the development of articulate
speech, the underlying mechanisms of empathy, insights into autism
and an understanding of the appeal of spectating at sports, dance or
dramatic performances. As well as this there is the issue of the effects
of electronic media, which resonates with many of the strands
already mentioned in this chapter.

An understanding of the emotional states of others is fundamental to
rational human behaviour. Understanding how empathy develops
and is formed will assist in shaping the behaviour of those who have
difficulty in this respect. Knowing how a deficiency in mirror neurons may be remedied could also help to develop our understanding
of autism. One preliminary study suggests that autistic children have
fewer mirror neurons (Bio-Medicine, America, 2007).

Mirror neurons and the acquisition of language

The discovery of mirror neurons opens up new possibilities in the
study of language development. It is likely to help us understand
more about how a child acquires language – possibly challenging
Chomsky's notion of an innate 'language acquisition device' – and

may shed light on the essential nature of the early spoken language exchanges that underpin the development of speech. Similarly, we may learn more about the difficulties that children who are exposed to too much television early on in their life experience:

> We are perhaps just beginning to comprehend our abilities with imitation. Although individuals are not replicators in the traditional sense, the fact that we are veritable copy machines in the wild is the key to understanding the development of human culture and to understand an unrecognized pervasive force of nature: the imitation factor. (Dugatkin, 2000)

Clearly, the value of children being able to listen to the language of significant people in their lives is essential. This has been well documented in many studies and particularly in the work of Gordon Wells and colleagues (Wells et al., 1981).

Modelling performance

The opportunity to imitate others as well as to visualise our own performance is important for success in the acquisition of new skills. The following extract from the work of the original researchers in this field shows how this works in practice.

> In all these experiments, however, the movements to be imitated were simple and highly practised. What role might mirror neurons play when we have to learn completely new and complex motor acts by imitation? To answer this question, Giovanni Buccino at our University, and collaborators in Germany recently used fMRI to study participants imitating guitar chords after seeing them played by an expert. While test subjects observed the expert, their parieto-frontal mirror neuron system became active. The same area was even more strongly activated during the subject's imitation of the chord movements. Interestingly, in the interval following observation, while the participants were programming their own imitation of the guitar chords, an additional brain region became active, known as pre-frontal area 46. This part of the brain is traditionally associated with motor planning and working memory. It may therefore play a central role in properly assembling the elementary motor acts that constitute the action the subject is about to imitate. (Rizzolatti, 2006)

The implication here is that the skills of attention need to be developed so that children can perceive the subtleties and complexity of movement to enable them to model and imitate the skills they wish to learn. Sometimes the best way to achieve the development of a skill is to have the opportunity to observe someone doing it well.

Imitation and young children's development

There is an excitement about the possibilities of discovery from this fast-emerging field, as is shown by this commentary on the importance of imitation:

> The time for studies of imitation has arrived. Imitation is readily studied at multiple levels by interdisciplinary research teams. It informs us about perception, motor control, the mechanisms underlying perception-action coupling and self-other relations. Over the next decade, it promises to become a prototypical case of interdisciplinary research on brain-behaviour relations and to shed light on both cognitive questions and those aimed at understanding intersubjectivity. (Meltzoff, 2002)

In one chapter, Meltzoff proposes that infant imitation is a precursor to developing empathy towards others and a theory of mind, and emphasises the importance of the quality of care and the environment in early childhood. He also raises issues about the impact of too much time spent watching television. Another expert, this time in the field of inter-subjectivity, suggests the importance of imitation for the social and intellectual life of infants:

> Matching another's actions may seek attention and provoke reply, accept or reject advances, express admiration or mockery. (Trevarthen, 2005)

He commends those working with young children to see how imitating and accepting imitations can help to build reciprocal confidence.

The propensity of young children to imitate is well known. Researchers in the 'How Babies Think' team noticed twenty-five years ago that one-month-old babies respond to facial expressions, including sticking their tongues out. In their research, they noted that babies as young as 42 minutes old possessed this same ability (Gopnik and Kuhl, 1999). They also noted that the 'theory of mind' developed early in life so that 'by the time we are five years old, we seem to understand the mind in much the way we will twenty or thirty years later'.

We already know a great deal about the role of imitation in language acquisition, but it seems that it also works well in reverse. Lise Eliot suggests that babies love the sense of control they get from being copied or imitated, and notes that studies of adoptive mothers show that imitation is the one type of interaction that best predicts their babies' verbal development at one year of age (Eliot, 2001).

 Point for reflection

> As it seems from the evidence that imitation is so vital for learning, how can you incorporate this into your work with the students you teach? What would you say you are already doing to help your students in terms of imitation and modelling?

The relevance of the arts for modelling and imitation

The skills of imitation may have even more important consequences than those mentioned thus far, if the predictions of the discoverers of mirror neurons are to be believed:

> Many aspects of imitation have long perplexed neuroscientists, including the basic question of how an individual's brain takes in visual information and translates it to be reproduced in motor terms. If the mirror neuron system serves as a bridge in this process, then in addition to providing an understanding of other people's actions, intentions and emotions, it may have evolved to become an important component in the human capacity for the observation-based learning of sophisticated cognitive skills. (Rizzolatti, 2006)

One of the prerequisites then for imitation is the need to attend and observe. This brings us back to the theme of attention, and to the debate about the special relevance of the arts in the curriculum where imitation and modelling should play a prominent role. There are many arguments for the importance of the arts in children's school experience, but in terms of the major themes in this chapter, we can also argue the importance of the arts for the brain. To put this into perspective, we need to be aware of the massive shift in the time children spend on out-of-school activities. Professor Marian Diamond provided these data from research in 1991 by the universities of Loyola and Illinois of children in 1,000 households:

- hobbies – 2 minutes;

- art activities – 4 minutes;

- out of doors – 8 minutes;

- reading – 8 minutes;

- passive leisure activities – 11 minutes;

- sport – 18 minutes;

- watching television – 124 minutes;

- in general play – 128 minutes. (Diamond, 1998)

The arts and sensory experience

Elliot Eisner presents compelling arguments not just for the inclusion of the arts in the curriculum, but for their integration as essential elements in connection with pupils' powers of attention:

> Today's students need arts education now more than ever. Yes, they need the basics, but today there are two sets of basics. The first – reading, writing and math – is simply the prerequisite for a second more complex, equally vital, collection of higher-level skills required to function well in today's world. (Eisner, 2002)

Eisner also presents finely-detailed arguments for the importance of sensory experiences, the very thing that is lacking from unmediated television watching:

> The sensory system is the primary resource through which the qualitative environment is experienced.

It is our sensory experience which provides the brain with the basic resources to make sense of our world.

In arguing the case for the role of the arts in cognitive development, he places the need for forms of 'representation' at the heart of his suggested practices. He sees the experience of representation as having profound consequences for the quality of mental life. Good arts teaching, he explains, helps children to perceive subtleties and to recognise complexities among the qualitative relationships encountered in the phenomenal world. Conceptual life he sees as operating from the sensory modalities and in 'their combination'. Put more simply, children need time to attend, observe and engage in the world with their senses. Over time, they need opportunities to represent their experience in a variety of possible forms. Eisner also talks of consciousness as the product of attention, and attention he says is based on past experience and moderated by current need or purpose. This is the crux of the argument for children:

> Because consciousness is based on sensibility, the refinement of the senses is of prime importance. (Eisner, 2002)

This development of the senses is necessarily based on sensory and direct experience of the world. Young children must have frequent opportunities to engage the world with their senses in order to differentiate, and thence to form, concepts. This process needs mediation through language and relationships with others, both children and adults. Moreover, research supports the notion that thought precedes language, that it is largely based on sensory experience, and that this experience is essential in early life:

> To learn language infants must develop a conceptual base onto which language can be mapped. Recent research in infant cognitive development shows that at least by nine months of age infants have developed a conceptual system sufficiently rich to allow language to begin. (Mandler, 2004)

There is also a further dimension concerning imitation and the notion of mirror neurons, as is noted by Blakemore and Frith:

> We are predisposed to imitate those around us and we are most likely to imitate those we admire. (Blakemore and Frith, 2005)

Teachers' and parents' values, beliefs and attitudes to learning can be as important in the learning process as the material being taught. The adults in a child's life are essential as role models, with the potential to add to and improve significantly a child's experience and understanding of learning.

Problem solving and the development of cognitive processes

A final point raised by Eisner in relation to this discussion is the importance of problem solving and the Bauhaus tradition, which originally combined crafts with the fine arts and an approach to design. He notes that this is alive and well in some schools.

> Such schools are oriented to meeting social needs; to do so they focus on invention, foster analytic abilities needed to figure out what will work and develop skill in the use of tools. (Eisner, 2002)

This kind of practice supports development from the intellectual foundations of observing, differentiating, conceptualising and representing that Eisner espouses, and this fits well with what we are learning about the brain and the vital importance of attention.

 Point for reflection

Imitation is an essential survival skill, and we tend to imitate those we admire. In what ways could we modify the curriculum to provide pupils with more opportunities to learn through imitation?

Learning from experience

John Dewey pointed out that:

> the belief that all genuine education comes from experience, does not mean that all experiences are genuinely or equally educative. (Dewey, 1938)

Sensory experience is of course an essential ingredient of attention, but so are the accompaniments of language, relationship, emotion and purpose. The illuminating work of the Israeli psychologist Reuven Feurstein clearly demonstrates the importance of 'mediated learning experiences'. His work shows the disadvantage and possible damage for children who lack adult guidance and support for their learning, and he stresses the importance of adult intervention and interaction in a child's learning:

> Our parents and relatives acting as the agents of culture, impose meaning on the stimuli that constantly bombard us, and in this way, ensure the transmission of values from one generation to another. Our senses alone cannot do this. (cited in Sharron, 1987)

The use of the term 'culture' here is specific to the traditions and values of groups who were separated from their original home backgrounds.

However, much of what Feurstein says applies to the children of today's television generation. He argues that a failure to transfer meanings to the younger generation can produce criminal and anti-social tendencies:

> Unsocialised or criminal behaviour is not radical or revolutionary, it is inadequate behaviour. (cited in Sharron,1987)

This may seem a tenuous connection, but it could well be one of the factors influencing the current increase in antisocial behaviour (see Palmer, 2006, 'Mind the Gap'). Certainly there is a connection with lack of attention as is seen in this description of a group of low-attaining children:

> They had enormous gaps in the cognitive processes or thinking skills which ordinary children pick up through interaction with their families. They found it hard to make comparisons between things and events, so that they could not reach conclusions based on comparisons; their perception was sweeping – it failed to differentiate items sufficiently to discover the difference between figures, shapes, patterns and letters. (cited in Sharron, 1987)

Feurstein describes these children as 'victims of information'; they simply have not learned how to master and use information creatively for either their school or daily lives. The same children improved dramatically with remedial teaching.

Instrumental Enrichment

'Instrumental enrichment' is the name for Feurstein's approach to remedial teaching. It presents a challenge to intelligence tests, the usual method of measuring and predicting intelligence. His main tenet is that children who are unable to learn from experience or to benefit from teaching may well be suffering from cognitive deficiencies, but it does not mean that they are unintelligent. If the impact of television and other electronic media is as dramatic as is claimed by the critics cited in this chapter, then more children may need the kind of help suggested by Feuerstein's approach than is currently the case.

'It's brilliant for your brains' is the response from one child to the instrumental enrichment programme (Sharron, 1987). An excellent version of the programme which offers suggestions for use in school community and home is contained in *Bridging Learning In and Out of the Classroom* (Skuy, 1999). It contains a range of exercises to teach what might be considered as the sub-skills that underpin the basic skills which children need for success in both school and life. These materials could also be used as the basis for assessment where there are concerns about levels of performance on entry to school.

First-hand and guided experience as the keystone for learning

Another approach to learning which is important to consider as a means for improving the attention skills of children both at home and at school, and which also links to the curriculum, is the notion of guided or first-hand experience. In the foreword of an important book devoted to promoting the practice of first-hand experience, Tim Smit, the founder of the Eden Project, provides a personal response to emphasise the value of this process:

> The most important single event in my sensory life was when a good friend asked me to give him one hour of my time to do exactly as he demanded. I trusted him and agreed. He took me to a field and marked out a metre square of grass. He made me sit and asked me to stare at it for a full hour, maintaining my concentration. To start with I saw grass. Then I saw a spider, then an ant, more ants, more spiders, beetles, a shrew, and within an hour, my world had turned upside down. I had looked through the keyhole at a micro-world heaving with life, all of it oblivious of me ... First-hand experience is the most important foundation stone in discovering who you really are and what you might become. (cited in Rich, et al., 2005)

It is clear from the evidence in this chapter that attention is fundamental to learning. Similarly, attention is supported by direct sensory experience, especially for young children. There is nothing new here. Both Rousseau and John Dewey laid an emphasis on learning from experience, and the Plowden Report also praised the use of the environment as a means of providing 'first-hand experience' (Department of Education and Science, 1967). Many schools today use first-hand experience as a conscious part of their curriculum approach (Macgilchrist, 2005). What is different now though is the understanding that attention and sensory experience are vital routes into brain development and that current lifestyles inhibit intellectual possibilities for some children.

First-hand experience and the Foundation stage of education

In the Froebel Project, Chris Athey, a much respected early years practitioner, confirmed the importance of first-hand experience that had previously been shown in the earlier Plowden Report. Here she emphasises the contribution made by visits and trips to enriching children's follow-up work:

> An analysis of the content of symbolic representations showed that sixty per cent consisted of objects and events in connection with visits. (Athey, 1990)

She continues by explaining that knowledge of the cognitive capacities of privileged and underprivileged children:

> strongly suggests that early enrichment has a cumulative effect in that subsequent experiences are amplified by enriched minds.

Her final suggestion is very much in line with the findings from this chapter. She advocates more accurate information for the effectiveness of schooling than testing at 7-years-old and the use of what has now become baseline assessment. In the future this assessment needs to take into account the quality of children's early experience, and the capacities for attention and the language which should accompany it. This would help to match the curriculum experience offered with each child's current abilities.

Athey provides a simple example. She describes Nicky, a 3-year-old in kindergarten, who is trying to sort out whether a drawing is of a cave or a cage. He says:

> But you can see it's a cage. Caves have got stalactites and stalagmites: they go up and down. A cage has got bars over the front. That's got bars over the front a cave hasn't got bars over the front. (Athey, 1990)

This level of discrimination would be impressive at any age. Here it reflects well on the adults involved who provided the guided experience and the language of explanation for Nicky's learning. Athey comments that:

> by the age of three, many of the kindergarten children were so widely experienced that it was difficult to detect their cognitive structures under an abundance of content.

In the findings of the Froebel project, and through the work of Reuven Feurstein, it is apparent that the opportunities for mediated or guided experience are crucial for a children's intellectual development. It is vital then to understand the maxim 'No attention – no learning'!

The constraints of National Assessment

The PACE Project, which investigated the impact of National Assessment procedures in primary classrooms, found that this kind of understanding and approach was not encouraged by an ever more rigid school context:

> Classrooms were increasingly strongly 'framed', in that teachers' discretion over how to teach was progressively diminishing and this structure was being relayed on to the pupils. Assessment was becoming increasingly categoric, regular and high stakes as requirements for accountability and performance measures became more prominent and explicit. (Pollard, 2000)

In addition, the authors argue that the most 'pervasive and significant' result of the policy agenda that was launched by the 1998 Education Reform Act was to reduce teacher and learner autonomy. One of the side effects of this was to reduce the number of educational visits – a very worrying development indeed, given the findings in this chapter.

Pupils' views of visits to places of interest

In the two surveys of children's attitudes to life and learning in school which we carried out during 2001–2004, the pupils themselves identified the importance of visits to places of interest being part of the curriculum. In the first survey of 300 pupils in an East London primary school, children were asked the question, 'If you were the teacher, how would you help children in your class to learn best?' Forty nine per cent chose the answer 'Take them out on trips'. This is a sizeable number of children picking up on a facet of their education they felt was neglected. Educational visits were happening less frequently, which was probably due to the increasing impact of the National Curriculum. Teachers felt less inclined to arrange trips, partly because of the pressure to cover content. At that time as well schools were feeling increasingly vulnerable to the possibilities of litigation, and were reluctant to take the risks involved in organising outdoor activities for children.

In another school in Tunbridge Wells, the teachers asked the pupils, 'What new places could we visit outside school to help with your learning?' Three children thought there was enough on offer, without specifying more. However, 320 children responded with a wide range of creative suggestions, including a visit to a 'chocolate factory' or just to 'another class'. All of the suggestions were purposeful, with the majority favouring museums, zoos and wildlife centres. In all there were some 40 different suggestions, reflecting considerable enthusiasm for experiences outside the classroom and for using the outside world to enhance learning.

In light of some of the evidence above, it may be time to reconsider the value of first-hand experience provided by schools through visits. This does not always mean elaborate journeys; sometimes carefully planned outings to local supermarkets, garages or shops can be just as rewarding. This is especially true for young children who may not have had much opportunity to attend and then reflect on their experience.

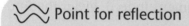 Point for reflection

There are times when the needs of young children and their carers seem to be in opposition. 'Take me out and show me things to talk about', the child might say. 'I have to get my work done', says the adult. Successful parents and teachers will find ways of attending to both. The right kinds of experiences will provide the nutrition for brain development and are absolutely essential.

Attention in the early years of life

The foundations of so many of our skills and attitudes are laid down from the very earliest stages of life. The ability to attend and focus is supported quite naturally by parents in a multitude of ways through showing objects and talking to their offspring. These early experiences are profoundly important as they connect attention, language and emotionally pleasurable events. Attention may be one of the first survival skills, but it needs practice to develop fully. Supporting the processes involved with attention 'enhances neural responses' and lays the foundations for sustained attention which become a vital mainspring in intellectual development. Expectations and aspirations are crucial here.

While working with some teachers on a course about our emerging understanding of learning and the brain, I heard one teacher declare that she had been taught at college that children could concentrate for only the same number of minutes as their chronological age. Unfortunately myths such as this persist unless challenged by the direct experience of observing children at work and at play. The pioneering work of Elinor Goldschmied shows in video format that young children (in this case 12–20 months old) have great powers of concentration and that they are perfectly able to sustain this for 20 minutes or more when the tasks provided are well matched to their interests (Goldschmied, 1992). One of the stipulations that she makes about the choice of materials – both for her 'treasure basket' containing materials for babies and her 'heuristic play' materials for older infants – is that they should be from the real world and not plastic. A metal egg whisk, a pewter pot, a lemon, a pine cone, are all preferable to highly coloured plastic. Her reason for this is that the natural materials provide better quality sensory experiences for children to engage with, and as we saw earlier, sensory experience provides a sound foundation for learning.

Goldschmied also provides a lot of excellent guidance to help parents and teachers take young children seriously as learners. When asked why the children respond with such high quality attention and concentration to her materials, she answers, 'They are making arrangements for their survival'. This is a wonderful encapsulation of much of what early experience and brain development are about. In one sense it goes with the grain of the brain, as infants are naturally curious in order that they can gain mastery of their environment for survival purposes. When children are keen to explore the world around them it is not just an add-on benefit – it is fundamental to life, learning and survival.

The key to these natural processes is the quantity and quality of adult support, and an attitude that supports rather than frustrates the infant's desire to gain mastery. Also important is the language that supports such experiences. Part of an infant's life should be dedicated to developing and extending their powers of attention, in the way that so many parents do. Look, look and look again – inquisitiveness is natural and necessary and sows the seeds for intellectual development. The role of adults is fundamental in helping children to sustain their attention, rather than simply following their impulses.

Moving to school

If parents and other caregivers have been acting as thoughtful coaches, children come into school with substantial experience stored in their brains as the basis for future learning. The task for the school then is to assess what children bring to the learning situation and to plan to take them forward. In a real sense, this is where 'personalised learning' begins.

The quality of children's early experiences before school is profoundly important in terms of their brain development. As Sue Palmer observes, attention is the first principle of learning; if a child cannot attend, then 'school will be problematic' (Palmer, 2006). It may be that many children will need help and practice with using their attention as a precursor to other curricular activities. As we have said before attention is a survival skill, but like all skills it improves with regular practice. Similarly, as Jane Healy observed, the role of the adult should be to help a child to use their pre-frontal cortex by putting thoughts and actions ahead of instant gratification. This approach will help them to avoid being stimulus-bound. If children can give attention and can manage the need for instant gratification, then the task of schools is made easier. If not, then schools will have to spend time teaching these sub-skills and the social underpinning which is also likely to be needed. The Plan-Do-Review structure used in many nursery schools and classes complements well the idea of children being less 'stimulus-bound'.

Guiding children's learning

Another aspect of Elinor Goldschmied's work with young children that is important here lies in finding the balance as teachers and parents between guiding learning and prescribing its course. When Elinor began working in inner-city nurseries, she found distress was the children's and adults' principle emotion. Anxiety over food, milk, biscuits and all of the daily routines of managing young children was manifest, but there was little emphasis on learning. She trained staff to let children explore the materials and learn in their own way and at their own pace. 'Here, let me show you' was considered anathema to the process of learning. Children need time to attend and to follow their own curiosity in order to develop the skills of sustaining interest. Put another way, in terms of brain growth, adults have to bear in mind the importance of the notion that 'the person doing the work is the one growing the dendrites and making connections in their brain' (Wolfe, 2001). This is a difficult concept for parents and teachers to adhere to, but if the learning is held to be paramount, then the role of guiding the learning, and not prescribing it, becomes clear.

A final point of great importance here is the use of direct experience at this stage in a child's learning journey. Making judicious opportunities for children's direct experience is an essential and continuous process for sensory learning and language acquisition. Every opportunity should be taken to use the immediate environment as the basis for curriculum experience, for in terms of learning for life

> the school should be less about preparation for life and more like life itself. (Dewey, 1938)

This is certainly what our brains need at all stages of life in school, but especially in the early years and at primary school.

Continuing in school

One of the basics about the brain is that it is greedy for oxygen, using up to one third of our intake. It should be so important to remember this in school, when so many bodies are crammed into relatively small spaces. How odd it seems, therefore, that while it is usual for nursery children to have almost continuous access to an outdoor area, where they can run and play in the fresh air, when they move across to a Reception class and become infants, their outdoor play is shoe-horned into a 15-minute break in the morning, with no more until lunchtime. As will be seen in the final chapter, there is substantial evidence to show that exercise is important for brain growth and development at all ages and stages of life. This evidence should be taken into account when planning the curriculum for young children – teachers need the freedom to give children regular 'brain breaks' for oxygen to refresh both their bodies and their brains.

Looking in depth

Children, and particularly young ones, need frequent opportunities to focus their attention on one thing at one time. It is true that we can multi-task and carry out different activities, but in terms of brain functioning there is a cost here in terms of efficiency. As we saw earlier in this chapter, we are better off doing one thing at a time in terms of sustaining our attention.

I recently watched a group of young children who had the task of investigating and defining 'Ten ways to describe a lemon'. They were given the opportunity and the time to cut up the lemon and use their senses to explore the taste, smell and texture, as well as its appearance and any other attributes. In time they were asked to provide a rank order of their choices and discuss their reasoning with a partner. Focusing their attention and looking in depth at one thing they were completely involved, showing a clear enjoyment and pleasure in what they were doing. This was a form of direct experience at its best, where the children were extending their sensory experience plus their knowledge and experience of what a lemon meant to them. This was not just an isolated event, but was built into a wider exploration of the senses through most aspects of the curriculum, including poetry, drama and music.

An excellent source of possibilities for first-hand experience is contained in *An Alphabet of Learning from the Real World* (Rich et al., 2005), a book referred to earlier in this chapter. Suggestions from it will provide starting points that can encourage direct or sensory experience, and will lead to sustained attention through interest.

The final section of this chapter provides connections with most of what has gone before on the theme of attention, by describing new research that identifies the learning skills that children take with them to school.

Learning from birth to three, with attention as the new formal discipline

A recent series of studies focuses on the brain functions that are crucial for learning in the first years of life (Posner and Rothbart, 2007). This is a very important work, as it provides new information about the earliest stages of learning development. It also confirms that attention is an essential skill for learning.

Attentional Networks

Posner and Rothbart ground their work in ten years of study on the themes of cognition and emotion using imaging with adults. This work led to the study of the identification of attentional networks in infancy. They presented objects in predictable positions to very young children, and recorded their eye movements throughout. The children were able to predict where the objects would be and could orient their attention to the correct place in anticipation of their appearance. However, if the objects were presented in unpredictable positions, the children encountered difficulties which they couldn't resolve. The ability to do this developed between the ages of two and three.

Posner and Rothbart considered that this ability was related to the activation of a high-level attentional network that regulated cognitive experience. Furthermore, the development of this network appeared to be a crucial step in the ability of children to regulate their own behaviours. They concluded that the ability to control attention was 'important in the child's adaptation to school and the ability to acquire the important skills of schooling'. (Posner and Rothbart, 2007)

Posner and Robart make three challenging and radical statements at the beginning of this ground-breaking work:

- The ability to learn literacy and numeracy appears to rest on the specific brain networks involved in these subjects, and also on attention networks, all of which are partly present prior to the start of formal schooling.

- Although in recent years parents and teachers have learned about the general importance of the first few years of life, they may not have realised the extent of the specific learning about language, number and attention that takes place. A combination of psychological and brain science studies has given us a window on the shaping of this knowledge early in life.

- Our view suggests that education should begin in infancy and involve a continuous, co-operative, enterprise between home and school in shaping the neural networks involved in school subjects. Parental knowledge of what is happening in the brains of their children can serve as the basis for enlisting a new level of involvement, at least from those parents most likely to be concerned with school achievement.

Attention as a core skill for learning

We have seen throughout this chapter how vital attention is for growth in the brain, and therefore for subsequent intellectual development. The evidence presented by Posner and Rothbart presents a new dimension of understanding about attention and its importance for learning, which is based on specific brain networks underlying performance. Attention involves these networks of the brain that mature from infancy well into childhood. The researchers point out, however, that 'attention also involves the regulation of the activity of other networks, thus improving the prospect of acquiring an unlimited number of skills'. They explain that attentional networks interact with other systems to establish priorities in perception and action, and show how the ability to regulate brain function makes attention relevant to all domains of learning. This leads to two important claims which justify the emphasis on attention suggested in this chapter:

- increases in attentional efficiency can influence progress in a wide range of school subjects;

- attention serves as a kind of formal discipline that can influence the efficiency of operations of a wide range of cognitive and emotional networks (Posner and Rothbart, 2007).

The dimension of temperament

There is a link here also with the emotions, the theme of the next chapter. The researchers argue that to do an effective job in teaching, it is necessary to take children's 'emotional and attentional characteristics' into account, and that these characteristics should be studied within the domain of what they describe as 'temperament'. They define temperament here as 'constitutionally based differences in reactivity and self-regulation' which have been observed within children's emotions, motor activity and attention. This derives from their view that individual differences in temperament constitute the earliest expressions of personality and the substrate from which later personality develops. Self-regulation is defined as those processes which modulate reactivity, including behaviour, avoidance inhibition and attentional self-regulation. Both these terms and the evidence base that underpins them are important for our understanding of the beginnings of learning – and for future success in school.

Focusing attention and the role of the caregiver

These ideas reflect new insights that come both from imaging and from careful observation of the earliest stages of the relationship between caregiver and child. For example, infants of three months old are virtually helpless, yet it is very important for their development that they have the ability to control where they look and what they attend to. This activity allows them to enter into their own education by selecting what interests them at the very earliest stages of development. Through their observations Posner and Rothbart have shown that a caregiver whose gaze is on the infant is more likely to attract his attention. They further contend that the basic mechanisms of attention are developing from three to six months, and that by 18 months infants are able to use the attention of the caregiver to enhance their education. They can, for instance, associate new words with objects that are in the direction of the speaker's attention (Baldwin, 1991).

Posner and Rothbart (2007) also touch on another aspect of attention – orienting, or the capacity of infants to be soothed when turning their attention towards novel objects – when they discuss the crucial role the caregiver plays in the child's emotional and cognitive development:

> Orienting can also momentarily soothe the infant. We believe that the caregiver's early involvement in the infant's learning, indicating where to move his or her eyes and moderation of the infant's emotions are critical steps on the road to self-regulation of emotion and cognition. Later, this system will be important for the development of the ability of the child to control their own cognition and emotions.

These statements concerning the gaze, orienting, novel objects and attention, all show just how important attention is for the range of essential skills that ultimately underpin success at school and in life. As Posner and Rothbart state in their summary:

> Socialisation builds on the natural tendency of infants to examine novel objects. It allows the caregiver, as a representative of the culture, to provide instruction on where to look … Our results suggest that the mechanisms guiding the implicit learning of where to orient are quite similar in four-month-olds and adults.

Attention training

Various forms of training to improve attention have been developed, some of them involving working with games on computers. Posner and Robart describe a different approach practised in Hungary, where attention-based activities happen in a social setting. Typical of these are 'eye-catching' exercises, where kindergarten children sit in a circle and have to catch the teacher's eye in order to leave the group, and other more sophisticated auditory and memory games for older children (Mills and Mills, 2000). These and other games are intended to improve children's listening and attention skills. Hungarian schools have a long history of high-quality and successful music teaching, and some of the practices described here could be valuable for children in this country.

They argue the case for a 'strong national priority' to adopt the best and most appropriate methods to assist all children in the important goal of self-regulation. In particular, they emphasise the importance of training attention in young children, citing evidence of successful training for five days with four- and six-year-old children that improved their attention networks and helped them to produce a more adult-like performance.

In the final section of their research, Posner and Rothbart describe how they tried to improve children's understanding of literacy and numeracy. They found that providing a web-based environment for teachers could be helpful with literacy learning and for preparing a 'linguistic environment designed to shape the auditory system in a way that will prepare for future reading' (Posner and Rothbart, 2007).

In the field of numeracy learning, they found that areas of the brain involving an appreciation of number are active with number-line functions during infancy. They also showed that the basic areas involved with comparing the quantity of numbers do not vary from five-year-olds to adults.

Posner and Rothbart believe that the ability to learn literacy and numeracy rests on the specific brain networks involved in these subjects, and also on attention networks. It is worth repeating again their conclusion when they argue that

> although in recent years parents and teachers have learned about the general importance of the first few years of life, they may not have realized the extent of specific learning about language number and attention that takes place.

The evidence from the studies in this chapter suggests that we need to take the whole issue of attention more seriously both at home and at school. It seems quite clear that attention is the foundation skill for most future learning, and that there is now a profound shift in our understanding of attention and how it affects learning.

Some implications for learners from the evidence considered in this chapter

- Young children need guidance from parents and teachers to focus and develop their skills with attention.

- Some children need help to inhibit activity in their other senses in order to focus on one sense.

- Children need encouragement to sustain their attention on activities, to counter the impact of technologies that provide mostly ephemeral experience.

- Children need to be taught how to use technologies for development as well as pleasure.

- Students need to understand the limits of multi-tasking in terms of what is happening in their brains.

- The strengths and weaknesses of watching television should be discussed with pupils.

- The importance of sleep for learners should be discussed, as well as the placing of technology in sleeping areas.

- Parents need guidance with understanding the importance of being physically active for learning, and particularly with regard to sport and the arts.

- Early sensory experience accompanied by language is vital for future learning.

- First-hand experience needs to be reinstated as a vital base for learning.

- The discovery of mirror neurons has important implications for learning.

- The process of joining school, especially via Nursery and Reception classes, requires sensitive discussion with parents as to the skills and experience that children possess and particularly as regards attention.

- The benefits and problems with television watching need to be discussed with parents as part of a home/school learning support policy.

In the next chapter, we will move on to the closely related theme of the emotions.

Here are four texts from the many referred to in this chapter that might be of particular interest for your further reading.

Toxic Childhood – Palmer (2006)

This is a well-researched book which covers most of the vital areas of childhood experience and looks at how the modern world is damaging our children and what we can do about it. The author doesn't sit on the fence and as a result tells a compelling story of what is happening to children socially and academically in British society and with reference to other countries in the developed world. She includes a survey of a group whose views are important, but not commonly heard – teachers. She found that more than 90 per cent of the 1000 people surveyed believed that children watch too much TV and have too little sleep.

Remotely Controlled – Sigman (2005)

This is a hugely important book by Professor Sigman who treads where others are reluctant to go and says what others fear to say regarding how television is damaging our lives and what we can do about it. Television is one of the gods that many of us worship today, and to criticise it is to invite derision or to be ignored. He observes that children now spend more time watching television than they spend in school – at present the average six-year-old will have spent nearly one full year of their life in watching TV, and will have had more eye-contact with television characters than their own parents. The reflection in the mirror is not pretty – he claims that TV stunts the development of children's brains and hinders educational progress, as well as contributing to many social problems such as violence, obesity and depression.

The Mind and The Brain – Schwartz and Begley (2002)

The authors (a professor of psychiatry and an award-winning scientific journalist) explore the phenomenon of Obsessive Compulsive Disorder (OCD). In so doing they describe the vital processes of attention which are central to their hypothesis and also to our understanding of learning. 'It is attention that makes neuroplasticity possible', they maintain. They find a powerful link between attention and the reversal of OCD through a four-step process. One of these steps involves mental rehearsal as a means for consolidating learning – a technique referred to in the next chapter. This leads to their conclusion that the mind can change the brain. 'We have been blinded to the power of the will to direct attention in ways that can change the brain.' Their interesting studies support the notion that we become largely what we attend to and focus upon.

As educators we need to appreciate more fully one of their closing comments:

Experience coupled with attention leads to physical changes in the structure and future functioning of the nervous system.

This statement illustrates where our understanding of learning is changing, with new insights into brain function.

Educating the Human Brain – Posner and Rothbart (2007)

The authors are renowned neuroscientists at the University of Oregon, who have worked together for twenty-five years. One of their main themes for collaboration is this study of child development and attentional networks. Their book is one of the most important works showing how neuroscience has relevance for education in the twenty-first century. It is quite technical in places, but this is necessary when breaking new ground for our understanding of the fundamentals of learning. The authors' passion for their subject matter shines through.

Learning and the emotions

A purely cognitive view of the mind, one that overlooks the role of the emotions, simply won't do! (Le Doux, 2002)

In the four sections of this chapter we will present evidence to support Le Doux's position. The main arguments in these sections will explore the interdependence of the emotions and cognition, and the essential role that the emotions play in the development of communication skills. In terms of the growth and development of the brain, we will see how the emotional support of a caregiver is essential to healthy brain function, and how the shaping power of a loving relationship is fundamental to sound development. Evidence for body and brain as an integrated system is presented, and the argument that the emotions should be an integral part of the curriculum is developed. Finally, we consider pupils' views of life and learning in school and the importance of their involvement in this process.

Here you will learn more about:

- how the emotions are vital for intellectual processes and the practice of learning;
- how relationships influence our physiological states and our sense of wellbeing, and how our first relationship (with mother or caregiver) profoundly influences our brain and our emotional development;
- how learning in the first two years of life is divided into two distinct stages, each vital in our preparation for lifelong learning, how the gaze between mother and infant is crucial both to communication and to attachment bonding, and how the expression of emotions can affect longevity;
- how emotions can help or hinder learning.

The power of the emotions

I was recently in a special school, helping nine year old Leroy with his maths. He was usually good at this subject, but all he could say in this lesson was 'I want to kill myself'. He kept repeating this phrase without any gestures or evident emotion and was largely unaware of my efforts to get him to focus on the task that he had started. In time his teacher, who had a really good relationship with him and understood his personal story well, managed to talk him round to the point where he became able to do the task.

This is an extreme case, but it points to the reality for some pupils whose lives and relationships have been and continue to be disrupted, and who need help to deal with their emotions in order to go forward with their learning. It also has relevance for all of us at one time or another, when powerful emotions take centre stage and other goals like learning become less important. As adults we can easily forget the sheer visceral power of strong emotions in children, so strong that their whole being can be dominated to the point of excluding everything else. If you were victimised or bullied as a child, it doesn't take much thinking about such experiences recreate the powerful feelings associated with them.

Our primary emotions, as agreed by most biologists and neuroscientists, include surprise, happiness, anger, fear, disgust and sadness (Le Doux, 1998). Le Doux asserts that these basic primary emotions constitute a list of the adaptive behaviours crucial to survival. Fear, for example, is clearly a necessary response to a threatening situation. The connection between the emotions and survival is essential to our understanding of the connections between emotions and learning, a point explored later in this section.

Walter Freeman (1999) explains how we can make sense of emotions by identifying them with the intention to act and noting their increasing levels of complexity. This is not surprising, for as many writers point out the word 'emotion' means a movement outwards. Thus action is very closely connected with motivation, which as Ratey notes is 'the process that ties emotion to action and ... decides how much energy and attention the brain and body assign to a given stimulus' (Ratey, 2001). This connection is important when we come to consider children's 'effortful action' when they first begin school. Some will be very focused while others will move around haphazardly without any apparent goals, this can indicate difficulty with attention (Posner and Rothbart, 2007).

Emotions and communication

Freeman makes a similar point:

> Emotions lie at the heart of our communication ... The important characteristics of emotions are those that well up from within the organism, and which are directed towards some future state, which is being determined by the animal in accordance with its perceptions of its evolving conditions and history. (Freeman, 1999)

These 'actions' at a more physiological level include the external expression of internal states of the brain. Many years ago Darwin identified some of these external expressions of emotion in social animals – panting, pawing, stamping the ground, erecting the hair or social organs, or moving the face or limbs (Darwin, 1872). Freeman continues by arguing that learning to communicate was essential for the survival of human groups, along with bodily motion and feeling. Thus learning and practice were required to perfect both the gestures that express emotions and their perception and correct interpretation. He shows how humans as social animals still have emotions at the heart of their communication:

> The most obvious fact of biological evolution in the past half million years is that the forms and dynamics of our brains and bodies have grown and adapted through social communication and interaction. (Freeman, 1999)

Le Doux agrees with this. Referring to Darwin once again in his major work on emotions (1998) he writes:

> For Darwin, an important function of emotional expression is communication between individuals.

Clearly then, from the perspective of the evolution of the brain, there is a vital connection between emotion and communication. Accountability, tests and league tables all focus on the outcomes of learning rather than the learning experience, and the importance that is currently attached to these in schools can make us forget the significant part that social communication continues to play in human learning.

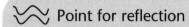

Point for reflection

Is it possible to make more time to talk with students about their feelings in regard to examinations and to discuss strategies for dealing with them?

The brain in three parts

In 1970, the neurologist Paul MacLean provided a unique and attractive explanation of where the emotions are located in the brain with his notion of the 'Triune Brain' (MacLean, 1990). He claimed that the brain is in three parts which have evolved over time. These consist of:

- the neo-cortex, the most recently formed part of the brain;

- the limbic or paleo-mammalian system;

- the reptilian brain, comprising the brain stem and cerebellum.

This hypothesis has become an influential paradigm that has brought about a rethink on how the brain functions. It had been assumed that the highest level of the brain, the neo-cortex, governed the lower levels. However, MacLean showed that the limbic system, with control over the emotions, could hijack the other levels when necessary. It is worth remembering here that while Susan Greenfield calls MacLean's work a 'revolutionary theory', not all neuroscientists are wholly supportive of his ideas (Greenfield, 2000). The main weakness, as Le Doux explains, is that:

> none of the enthusiasts for the limbic system have been able to identify what parts of the brain actually make up the limbic area. (Le Doux, 1998)

Nevertheless, as a working hypothesis, the notion of the 'Triune Brain' has generated some powerful ideas. Some of the most important of these in connection with learning and the emotions are described by three American psychiatrists in their original and contentious work, *A General Theory of Love* (Amini et al., 2000). They present powerful and passionate arguments for reassessing the importance of the emotions in our lives, particularly with regard to the welfare and education of children.

We now move on to reflect on some of these arguments, and the long-lasting effects that lack of love and neglect of the emotions can have on the growing child.

A general theory of love

Amini and his colleagues claim that:

> our society underplays the importance of the emotions. Having allied itself with the neocortical brain, our culture promotes analysis over intuition and logic above feeling. Cognition can yield riches, and the human intellect has made our lives easier in ways that range from indoor plumbing to the Internet. But even as it reaps the benefits of reason, modern America ploughs emotions under – a costly practice that obstructs happiness and misleads people about the nature and significance of their lives. (Amini et al., 2000)

In their review of the historical study of the place of emotions, they refer to the work of Darwin and a student of his work, Paul Ekman. The latter was a pioneer in connecting emotions with facial expressions. They note how Darwin's ideas were relegated to obscurity for decades until Ekman's work revealed that emotional expressiveness equips human beings with a sophisticated communication system. This, they assert, then led researchers in the mid-Sixties to the discovery of an emotional science based on Darwin's concept of emotion as a heritable neural advantage (Darwin was the first scientist to devote himself to the study of the emotions). (Ekman, 2003)

However, Amini et al. first revisit and develop MacLean's notion of the Triune Brain. In order to show the importance of the emotions in the human brain, they tell the story, (familiar in neurological literature) of the rail worker Phineas Gage. In 1848, an explosion drove a steel bar through the skull of the unfortunate Gage. It entered below his left eye and exited from the top of his head, taking a sizeable piece of his neo-cortex, and his reasoning faculty, with it. After the accident, Gage was a changed man. Although he could eat, breathe, sleep, talk and move about normally, he was now disorganised and slothful, which was in complete contrast to his former self. The point Amini et al. are making here is that had the blast sent the spike hurtling through Gage's reptilian brain he would have been dead before he hit the ground, because it is the reptilian brain that controls the life-preserving functions. It doesn't, however, have an emotional life. Lizards and other reptiles are cold-blooded, whereas the mammals which evolved from small lizard-like reptiles are warm-blooded, and they have different ways of functioning. The key distinction between the two parts of the brain is reflected in the profound evolutionary differences between mammals and reptiles.

The limbic brain

The limbic or mammalian brain is essentially different from the reptilian brain. Mammals, as noted by Amini and colleagues, live in close-knit social groups, and bear live young, nursing and defending them while they are immature. They will risk, and sometimes even lose, their lives to protect their young.

The finer details of nursing and comforting a baby were brought home to me recently on a visit to a department store. I watched a young mother with her newly-born baby in a sling over her shoulder, lying against her left side. The mother was standing and looking around the store and, almost unconsciously, she was kissing the baby and putting its hand in her mouth, providing continuous touch and affection. I later found out that most mothers intuitively put their babies on the left side, and because of this the baby can hear their heartbeat. I was moved by the quantity and quality of the constant physical contact and reassurance that she gave to the child. It was a touching reminder of the essential need that humans have to give and receive physical contact and love.

Movement and the brain

Amini et al. finally turn to the neo-cortex, the largest and most recently acquired part of the human brain. They note its importance for the amazing feats of co-ordination that underlie the simplest act, such as reaching to pick up a cup of coffee. Movement requires a larger brain and they point out earlier in their book that bacteria, a highly successful life form, possess no brain at all. An interesting anecdote that supports this view is told by Susan Greenfield (1997). The late Emperor Hirohito, a passionate student of marine biology, observed the sea squirt. When this creature is immature it has a small brain, needed in order to swim around in the sea. When it matures, however, it stops moving about and attaches itself to a rock, where it lives by filtering sea water. It no longer needs to move, and so consumes its own brain! This observation illustrates that the brain is essential to control movement. It also acts as a reminder that, just as the emotions are central to learning, movement too is important, even though at our present level of knowledge we may not be able to see the particular relevance (Hannaford, 1995).

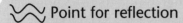 Point for reflection

How can teachers and parents provide more opportunities for movement as part of children's learning experiences?

The neo-cortex is, however, concerned with much more than just movement. Human beings have the largest neo-cortex to brain ratio of any creature, a proportion that confers on us our capacity to reason, use symbols and work with abstraction. When they reflect on the generally accepted notion of the supremacy of the neo-cortex, the writers of *A General Theory of Love* move to their main criticisms of American society and the problems that they feel are accruing there, particularly with regard to the care and wellbeing of children.

The shaping power of love

They express their concerns at a social level:

> Without limbic resonance, a child doesn't discover how to sense with his limbic brain, how to tune in to the emotional and understand himself with others ... Children thus handicapped grow up to become fragile adults who remain uncertain of their identities. Anxiety and depression are the first consequences of limbic omissions. (Amini et al., 2000)

This form of neglect or omission can have serious consequences for the individual and for society. The perceived need for what the authors term 'limbic regulation' – essentially an abundance of unconditional love and relationship – leads them to the dire conclusion that 'a limbically damaged human is deadly'. If the neglect is sufficiently profound, they see the result as 'a functionally reptilian organism armed with the cunning of the neocortical brain'. Their grim analysis continues with the prediction that if nothing changes in the pattern of bringing up children, such violence will emerge from even younger 'lethal' children.

Unconditional love

The path that they follow to reach these conclusions covers some familiar territory. They revisit the work of the ethologist Konrad Lorenz, the analyst Rene Spitz, and the psychologist Harry Harlow. They conclude, particularly from Harlow's work with monkeys in the 1950s, that 'love and the lack of it change the young brain forever'. This conclusion derives from several studies, with one concerning animals being particularly noteworthy. Researchers placed monkey mothers and infants in an environment where food was not easily available. This situation eroded the mothers' parental attentiveness, and their distracted behaviour patterns created despair and anxiety reactions in their infants. When the infants grew into full adults, an analysis of their brains was carried out which showed permanent alterations in their brain chemistry. (Harlow, 1958) The outcomes from this and similar work led Amini et al. to conclude that limbic regulations are not only life-sustaining, but fundamentally essential to life itself.

In conclusion, these three psychiatrists challenge the supremacy accorded to the neo-cortex in our contemporary thinking:

> To the neo-cortical brain, rich in the power of abstractions, understanding makes all the difference, but it doesn't count for much in the neural systems that evolved before understanding existed.

Love matters in the life of a child

Amini et al. combine their joint experience in consultancy, their insights from poetry and their understanding of neuroscience, to argue for a greater emphasis on sustained relationships to make a more stable society. They offer a view of relationship which is far deeper and more interdependent than is generally conceived:

> In relationship, one mind revises another; one heart changes its partner. This astounding legacy of our combined status as mammals and neural beings is limbic revision: the power to remodel the emotional parts of the people we love. Who we are and who we become depends, in part, on whom we love. (Amini et al., 2000)

Central to this statement is the concept of physiological interdependence, which can seem counter-intuitive to a philosophy based on individualism. We normally feel that as individuals we are in control of our lives and our bodies, but Amini et al. present an alternative view here:

Because human physiology is at least in part an open loop arrangement, an individual does not direct all of his own functions. A second person transmits regulatory information that can alter hormone levels, cardiovascular function, sleep rhythms, immune functions and much more inside the body of the first.

This notion of individual development as interdependent is profoundly challenging, because it makes relatedness and communal living the centre of human life – 'The unimpeachable verdict: love matters in the life of a child' (Amini et al., 2000).

As we shall see, evidence from studies of the first two years of life shows that love matters hugely for learning too.

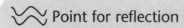 Point for reflection

Although these ideas are contentious for some, what would the implications be for a school or community of learners to act on the principles of interdependence in learning and behaviour? How would pupils and teachers feel about acknowledging their dependence on each other?

The emotional brain

Returning to the theme of the Triune Brain which has contributed so much to the creative thinking of Amini et al., it has to be noted that many neuroscientists find the theory or hypothesis useful but nevertheless express reservations. This view is well captured by Joseph Le Doux who is highly respected for his work on the emotions. He observes that MacLean's emphasis on evolution as the key to understanding the emotions is 'just about perfect', but also holds that MacLean is mistaken to wrap up the entire emotional brain and its evolutionary history into one package (Le Doux, 1998).

If MacLean's emphasis on the emotions and evolution is so apt, then perhaps we need to give this more prominence in our consideration of the education of children in the twenty-first century. (The issues described in this section apply as much to the UK as to the USA.) A current report about childhood carried out by UNICEF in 21 industrialised countries covered six dimensions, including the quality of children's relationships and their wellbeing. The UK and the USA were placed at the bottom of the rankings.

There is also anecdotal evidence which supports these findings. Recently in the UK we have witnessed a spate of shootings and knifings where young people have died. There was also a case reported in the media where four women goaded two toddlers to fight. They allegedly laughed as they videoed a two-year-old boy in a nappy being hit by his sister of three years old. At the very least this action betrays a complete lack of understanding of relationship and emotions on the part of these women, but it also points to a growing problem in our society where our emotional lives are often misunderstood or ignored.

These are social issues which affect us all, but they have a particular influence on the whole process of education through the kinds of experience children bring with them into school. The previous chapter described the importance of attention, the impact on it of watching television from an early age and the consequent lack of readiness in many children for the process of learning. Even more significant is the quality of emotional experience that children bring with them in terms of their ability to take advantage of what school has to offer. The importance of how children are received into school and the sensitive assessments that can be made in conjunction with parents will be dealt with in Chapter 6.

 Point for reflection

If, as the writers of *A General Theory of Love* argue, the importance of our emotions is largely ignored in education, at what points and in what ways could we begin to include them more as part of the curriculum?

How attachment and self-regulation shape the brain in the early years of life

The past fifteen years have seen a wonderful sea change in the field of child development. This change has been brought about through patient scholarship using imaging techniques in interdisciplinary research, including the study of neurobiology and the emotions. John Bowlby provided the foundation for these changes, particularly in his seminal text *Attachment*. Written in 1969, this established the basic tenets of attachment, which he defined as a tendency in children from birth to three years of age to maintain proximity to an attachment figure.

The focus of attachment now is more closely based on the relationship between caregiver and infant in the first three years of life. The research and writing of Allan Schore are central to the new insights into our understanding of how the brain is shaped during these early stages of life. In the preface to his major work, *Affect Regulation and the Origins of Life*, he explains that:

> The beginnings of living systems set the stage for every aspect of an organism's internal and external functioning throughout the lifespan. (Schore, 1994)

'Affect' in this context (and in this book generally) is taken to mean the conscious subjective aspect of feeling or emotion.

In a more recent work, Schore explains further that:

> the concept of regulation is one of the few theoretical constructs that is now being utilized by literally every developmental discipline. (Schore, 2003)

'Regulation' here is taken to mean, as Damasio suggests, 'the control of the emotions' which is essential to the adaptive function of the brain (Damasio, 1994).

The first nine months of life outside the womb

Schore reminds us that although there is widespread agreement that the brain is a self-organising system, there is less appreciation of the fact that the self-organisation of the developing brain occurs in conjunction with another brain – that of the caregiver. Here then is the focus for this profoundly important work, a deeper understanding of what is taking place between infant and caregiver during the first months of life outside the womb.

From the moment of birth, the primary caregiver plays an essential role which at its least encompasses:

- shaping the maturation of structural connections within the cortex;

- shaping the limbic areas that create social and affective functions;

- regulating the infant's psychobiological states;

- assisting life-sustaining functions of fluid balance and temperature regulation that eventually become self-regulating;

- providing sensitive and varied affective experiences;

- developing psychobiological systems for homeostatic regulation;

- establishing the chemical transmissions that identify pleasure with a social relationship. (Schore, 2003)

Shaping the brain

Schore explains how these earliest psychosocial contacts involve sensory experience, in particular warmth. By the second quarter of the first year, myelination of the occipital areas of the cerebral cortex occurs, and thus vision comes into play. Myelination is the development of a wax-like sheathing around the nerve fibres which allows tiny electrical communications to pass between nerve cells. These in turn enable a particular type of visual information exchange which conveys a mother's affective responses to her infant and results in synchronous changes in both the child's and mother's states. Turner, exploring the origins of emotions, suggests how this important development of the visual cortex evolved:

> One selection pressure was for better vision. Unlike most mammals that are olfactory dominant, higher primates are visually dominant. Primate brains have been rewired to subordinate other sensory inputs – haptic, auditory, and even olfactory – to vision. (Turner, 2000)

The synchronous gaze and dance

Over the first year of life, visual experiences are of great significance, with a mother's emotionally expressive face and eyes being the most potent image. The infant's gaze stimulates the mother's gaze and creates a dyadic (2-person) system in which the most intense inter-personal communication takes place. The mother attunes to the infant's state and changes the intensity and duration of her affective stimulation to maintain the child's positive state. The more the mother tunes her activity level to the infant during periods of social engagement, and the more she allows him to recover quietly in periods of disengagement, the more synchronised their interaction becomes (Schore, 2003). Schore also observes:

> In synchronized gaze, the dyad creates a mutual regulatory system of arousal in which both move together. (Schore, 2003)

In other words the bond is so powerfully formed that they almost become a single working unit. These dialogues between mother and child increase over the second and third quarter of the first year and form the basis of bond formation. This relationship is exquisite – like a beautiful and elaborate dance of life.

This dance is described from a different perspective in the influential work of Colwyn Trevarthen. He describes the foundations of speech through maternal-infant proto-conversation, and concludes, that:

> the affective regulations of brain growth which is embedded in an intimate relationship, promotes the development of cerebral circuits. (Trevarthen, 1996)

The right cortex is known to be influenced by early social experience and to be activated in intense states of elation. Schore reports that the child uses the output of the mother's emotion-regulating right cortex as a means of imprinting the hard wiring of circuits in his own right cortex to mediate his own growing affective capacities (Mortimore, 2006).

Mother love and endorphins

Many chemical changes take place in the brain in the first year of life through interactions between child and mother. The mother's face triggers high levels of endogenous opiates (chemicals from within the infant brain), and these provide rewards for social interaction, social effect and attachment. Maternally-induced and increasing amounts of dopamine and endorphins (chemicals that produce feelings of pleasure) then mediate the experience of enjoyment in the child.

Life dependency

In summary, at this stage:

> It is the emotional availability of the caregiver in intimacy which seems to be the most central growth-promoting feature of the early rearing experience. (Mortimore, 2006)

Similarly, Krystal (1988) concludes that:

> the development and maturation of affect-feelings, represents the key event in infancy. (Schore, 1999)

It is hard to overestimate how important these early processes are for the whole of a person's life.

> The non-verbal, pre-rational stream of expression that binds the infant to its parent continues throughout life to be a primary medium of intuitively felt affective-relational communication between persons. (Orlinsky and Howard, 1986)

These observations about the importance of the mother-child relationship should give us serious pause for thought, especially in light of the large increase in the number of very young mothers. For example, in one London borough between 1995 and 1997 there were 89 conceptions per 1000 girls aged 15 to 17. Taken with the evidence in this chapter, it seems of the highest importance to provide every support for these young women in order that they many fulfil their role with an understanding of the subtle yet vital nature of the mother-infant relationship. In fact, the whole issue of maternity needs higher status. One recent survey of 5000 mothers found that 20 per cent of them felt unsupported during labour, and a high percentage complained of 'poor quality, depersonalised care' (Elliott, 2007). Support for young mothers is thus a crucial issue for both the present and the future.

∿ Point for reflection

The evidence illustrating the essential nature of the relationship between mother and child for both wellbeing and brain development cannot be ignored. How can this information be made available in sensitive and responsible ways that do not increase the levels of guilt that some mothers already feel?

Separation

Towards the end of the first year, the neo-toddler moves towards autonomy and begins to separate himself from his mother in order to explore the non-maternal environment. The experiences of separation and reconnection with the mother enable the child to be exposed to an enriched environment, one that shapes brain networks and increases neural connections. So:

> At 10 months, 90% of maternal behaviour consists of affection, play and care-giving. In sharp contrast, the mother of the 13- to 17-month-old toddler expresses a negative on average every 9 minutes. In the second year, the mother's role will change from a caregiver to a socialization agent, as she must now persuade the child to inhibit unrestricted exploration, tantrums, bladder and bowel functions, ie, activities that he enjoys. (Schore, 2003)

The developing brain and the orbito-frontal cortex

It is around this time, as Sue Gerhardt observes, that the pre-frontal cortex assumes its unique role:

> It links the sensory areas of the cortex with the emotional and survival-oriented sub-cortex. (Gerhardt, 2004)

The orbito-frontal cortex (OFC) also becomes important now, as it is critically involved in the attachment process. It is found behind the eyes, close to the amygdala. The region of the OFC is involved in social and emotional behaviours and the self-regulation of body and emotional states. Its importance is particularly apparent when it is damaged, as it can lead to an inability to relate to others sensitively, and to respond to social and emotional cues. Notably, the OFC controls the right hemisphere which is dominant in the early years of life. Perhaps the significance of this form of development can be more easily understood using the work of Chugani et al. in their study of Romanian orphans (Chugani et al., 2001).

The painful effects of a lack of love and care

Chugani and his team studied ten Romanian orphans, using positron emission tomography (PET) scans to examine brain dysfunction. They were aware from previous studies of the effects of early global deprivation, where infants were left for up to 20 hours per day unattended (Ames and Carter, 1992; O'Connor and Rutter, 2000).

Chugani et al. found that the children showed an altered development of limbic structures, including the orbito-frontal cortex, and concluded that those who had been exposed to early social deprivation showed evidence of those long-term cognitive and behavioural deficits associated with brain dysfunction.

These sad outcomes will not be a surprise to those in the caring professions. Some very positive and thoughtful guidance has been made available to help practitioners, following a review of provision in Scotland. The Scottish Executive Education Department (SEED) commissioned Professor Colwyn Trevarthen and a team of colleagues to consider the research evidence on the development of children from birth to three years old. The guidance they produced includes the following suggestions for provision for infants up to three months old:

Guidance for the care of children nought to three years

- Adults should regulate the intensity of emotion experienced by the infant, calming or stimulating by affectionately holding, touching and talking with them.

- Carers should help to develop an active and purposive state of mind in the baby by mirroring their emotions and sharing attention to objects and people.

- Each infant should be cared for by one adult who becomes attuned to that child.

- Consistent care should be offered in a quiet, secure environment with opportunities for rest. Immediate responses to distress or expressions of need and a familiar playful and companionable intimacy are important. (Gregson, 2007)

This is one example of guidance which shows an understanding of the new research and insights into the early care and growth of infants. In addition, it helps to dispel the myth that infants need to learn to be sturdy little bodies and must suffer to become independent. As Gerhardt explains:

Often, parents are in such a hurry to make their child independent that they expose their babies to long periods of waiting for food or comfort, or long absences from the mother in order to achieve this aim … Unfortunately, leaving a baby to cry or to cope by himself for more than a very short period usually has the reverse effect. (Gerhardt, 2004)

Gerhardt also cites the paradox that underpins all human experience, which is that people need to have a satisfying experience of dependency before they can become truly independent and self-regulating. This also applies to the attitudes of the learner.

Learning and the second year of life

Learning is of course taking place from the start of life, but in a child's second year, when the mother's role changes, a secure emotional attachment facilitates the transfer of regulatory capacities from caregiver to infant. In the last half of the second year the final maturation of the orbito-frontal cortex takes place, which modulates and regulates the main elements of the developing limbic system. Eventually, through research, we are going to see more clearly how the relationship between emotion and cognition influences learning and how integrated the two are. A recent work by two highly respected neuroscientists, mentioned frequently in this book, gives important pointers in this direction (Posner and Rothbart, 2007).

We have now seen that the first two years of life are of vital importance to the shaping of the brain. This shaping occurs in the relationship between mother and child, largely through their emotional exchanges. We have also seen that there is emerging evidence about early emotions and cognition which has implications for schooling. In addition, individual differences in attention and affect seem to be important with regard to readiness for schooling. We now move on to consider the brain and the body as an integrated system, because this also bears on our ability to learn.

I feel therefore I am: brain and body – an integrated system

Having seen a little of how the emotions between infant and mother provide the very foundation of the brain through physical love and chemistry, it is apparent that the brain and the body are completely interdependent. Antonio Damasio puts this case very clearly.

> The brain and body are indissociably integrated by mutually targeted biochemical and neural circuits. (Damasio, 1994)

Almost every part of the body can send signals to the brain through nerves and chemicals. In a more recent work, he takes a step further when he says:

Work from my laboratory has shown that emotion is integral to the processes of reasoning and decision making, for worse and for better. (Damasio, 1999)

He also explains that we feel our emotions consistently and we are aware that we feel them. He describes how our minds and our behaviour are woven around continuous cycles of emotions, followed by feelings that create new emotions:

A running polyphony that underscores and punctuates specific thoughts in our minds and actions in our behaviour.

Finally he acknowledges that we can educate our emotions but we cannot entirely suppress them, and the feelings we have inside ourselves are testimony to our lack of success. In his research with patients, he became intrigued by the possibility that problems with reasoning were not primarily cognitive, but due to a defect in emotion and feeling. Over time he concluded that there were many ways in which

emotion and feeling were not merely players in the process of reasoning, but indispensable players. (Damasio, 2003)

In terms of the mind/body problem relationship which impinges on our views of learning, he proposes the following connections:

- the body and brain form an integrated organism;

- brain activity assists the regulation of human life;

- the brain functions for survival;

- the brain's regulatory operations depend on the creation and manipulation of mental images in the mind;

- these images include visual, auditory, tactile, olfactory and gustatory evidence;

- the interface between the body and these images causes a process of mapping;

- the structures in which the maps are formed are influenced by other brain structures. (Damasio, 2003)

In summary, the brain and mind are integrated and inseparable, or as Damasio puts it:

> body, brain and mind, are manifestations of a single organism.

If we accept his critique, then the body as well as the emotions needs to be taken into account when planning educational experiences.

The mind in the body

Another popular writer and fellow neuroscientist, Candace Pert, makes clear the connections between emotions and learning in her work concerning the function of peptides. A peptide is a chemical compound made up of two amino acids and it is usually smaller than a protein. At the time of her research, 88 of these had been identified. She explains that, just as drugs can affect what we remember, neuro-peptides can act as ligands or binding agents:

> to shape our memories as we are forming them and put us back in the same frame of mind when we need to retrieve them. (Pert, 1997)

She also sees the body and mind as one system:

> We are all aware of the bias built into the Western idea that the mind is totally in the head, a function of the brain. But your body is not there just to carry around your head. I believe the research findings I have described indicate that we need to start thinking about how the mind manifests itself in various parts of the body and, beyond that, how we can bring that process into consciousness.

She is even more radical in her thinking when considering 'bodymind'.

> Mind doesn't dominate body, it becomes body – body and mind are one. I see the process of communication we have demonstrated, the flow of information throughout the whole organism, as evidence that the body is actually the outward manifestation, in physical space, of the mind.

 Point for reflection

The evidence here powerfully suggests the need to connect the body and mind in the learning process. What are the implications for the age groups that you work with? Which of the practices that you use already take this into account?

The body as the theatre for the emotions

Pert's definition is close to the concept of the body as the 'theatre of the emotions' as expressed by Damasio:

> All emotions use the body as their theatre of internal milieu, including visceral, vestibular and musco-skeletal systems. However emotions also affect the mode of operation of numerous brain circuits. (Damasio, 1999)

Finally, Pert asserts her belief that:

> repressed emotions are stored in the body – the unconscious mind – via the release of neuro-peptide ligands and that memories are held in their receptors. (Pert, 1997)

This is perhaps a more controversial claim, but I found some support for it when working with headteachers on problem solving of the kind that their pupils had to do during SATs. Some heads had marked emotional responses to mathematical and other problems which must have been stored since they were at school. As some of them became quite anxious and even on occasions angry, I did wonder about their agitated and distressed body language and whether these experiences were at least partly stored in the body.

The field of 'bodymind' is being developed in biology into hitherto unseen areas. The work of Candace Pert has been extended by Bruce Lipton, who claims that the functional units of life are the individual cells of the body:

> Though every cell is innately intelligent and can survive on its own when removed from the body, we really represent the cooperative effort of a community of perhaps fifty trillion single cells. (Lipton, 2005)

He weaves into his theory the power of the subconscious mind and the influence of the study of epigenetics. This recently emerging field shows how the parental life experience shapes a child's genetic character. Although it is a long shot, this field may help us to understand more about the effects on children from different cultures, and those whose families who are long-term unemployed, with regard to learning (Lipton, 2005).

〰️ **Point for reflection**

At the heart of the new field of epigenetics is the idea that genes have a memory. So, 'the lives of your grandparents – the air they breathed, the food they ate, even the things they saw, can directly affect you decades later, despite your never experiencing these things yourself' (BBC, 2007). What are the possible implications that the disposition towards learning for some pupils may be influenced by their forebears, for example through long-term unemployment?

The emotions and longevity – the Nun Study

Another facet of the emotions and their impact on the body was explored in a study of a community of nuns from Minnesota in the USA begun in 1986 (Snowdon, 2001). Originally there were 670 nuns over seventy-five years of age. This longitudinal research was designed as an epidemiological study to attempt to gain more understanding of Alzheimer's disease and various aspects of aging. The community was an ideal population for the study, with three basic sources of data available about the participants. First, convent archives provided information about potential early- and middle-life risk factors for Alzheimer's. Second, annual examinations documented changes in the cognitive and physical function of each participant during old age. Third, because each sister agreed to brain donation, the structure and pathology of the brain could be related to early- and mid-life risk factors and to late-life cognitive and physical function.

Feelings for life!

Dr Snowdon and his team also considered the impact of the emotions and in particular whether there was any relationship with longevity. They were already aware of research from the Mayo Clinic in Rochester, Minnesota, which had followed 839 patients who had been classified as optimists or pessimists. In that particular study, thirty years after the original tests significantly more optimists than pessimists were still alive.

When the sisters joined the convent, at an average age of twenty-two, they were asked to write an autobiography. The researchers took these and analysed them according to a number of criteria, one of which was positive or negative emotions. The team were amazed to find that positive emotional content strongly predicted those who would live the longest lives. The results appeared like this:

Number of positive emotion sentences	Age at death
Fewest	86.6 years
Second group	86.8 years
Third group	90.0 years
Most	93.5 years

The ability to express positive emotions appeared to account for a survival difference of almost seven years. Further, the team found that the sisters who scored the lowest number of positive-emotion sentences had twice the death risk at any age when compared with those in the highest group. In their account, Snowdon says:

> the real question is; does a positive outlook in early life contribute to longevity? Our data suggests that the answer is yes. (Snowdon, 2001)

Talking of feelings

A valuable model for encouraging pupils to talk about their feelings is provided by Daniel Goleman in his descriptions of work with the 'Self-Science' curriculum (Goleman, 1995). From this it seems likely that children who grow up with caregivers who are comfortable in talking about and expressing their emotions behave in a similar way as they grow up, and are less at the mercy of their emotions than those who lack this experience.

Goleman describes successful practices for helping pupils from difficult home backgrounds to manage their emotions in productive ways by using self-knowledge.

 Point for reflection

How can we encourage pupils at different ages to express their emotions in such a way as to promote their learning?

Education for life

The Nun Study also confirms the data from other work concerning the correlation between education and life expectancy. The researchers found that those sisters with a college degree had a much better chance of surviving into old age. Because of the uniqueness of the study population, the team was able to rule out variables from previous studies where it was thought that the less educated were more likely to smoke cigarettes, earn less money, receive sub-standard health care and live in shabby housing. The sisters naturally had similar lifestyles, irrespective of their education or earlier privileges. Despite this, however, the better-educated sisters still had a lower risk of death at every age, so strengthening the probability of a connection between levels of education and life expectancy.

One final point concerning education from the study comes in the area of early learning. Snowdon and his team were surprised when presenting their findings at public gatherings as the same question came up time and time again: 'What does all this mean for our children?' 'Read to them' was Snowdon's reply. He explained that idea density, that is the number of individual ideas per ten words of writing, depends on two important learned skills – vocabulary and reading comprehension – and he argues that they are best learned earlier in life (Snowdon, 2001).

There are a further two factors that combine the themes from this and the previous chapter – attention and emotion. The act of reading to a young child not only provides enjoyment, but also demonstrates parental attention. Equally, the act of cradling a young child as part of reading is also a demonstration of love.

Fear and emotions for learning

It was William James who said that nothing marks the ascendancy of man from beast more clearly than the reduction of the conditions under which fear is evoked (*Principles of Psychology*, 1890). For a variety of reasons school is associated with fear for some pupils, so it is important to understand more about this emotion and its possible impact on learning. Fear is evidently a vital element of our survival strategies, and it has been argued that:

> it is the most primal emotion in all animals, as it is essential for the avoidance of danger and predation. (Turner, 2000)

Fear exists and must therefore be acknowledged as part of life and learning in school – and dealt with where possible.

Emotions and the amygdala

The neuroscientist and writer Joseph le Doux, who has done so much to help us to understand more about the emotional workings of the brain, notes that although 'we are evolution in progress', it is still the case that the amygdala has a greater influence on the cortex than the other way round (Le Doux, 1998). This small, almond-shaped area has the capacity to take a direct route to the brain in an emergency and trigger survival mechanisms such as increased heart rate and blood pressure, and heightened senses ready for action. Under normal circumstances without an emergency, signals sent through the cortex provide a more considered and rational response to a situation. Clearly, any act in school short of an emergency that causes the amygdala to react will put a student at a serious disadvantage for learning.

However, the impact of the emotions in general presents a more complex picture. The following notes on a molecular approach to the emotions acts as a warning against too simple an analysis (Howard, 1994):

- Each emotion seems to have unique physiological responses: for example, anxiety leads to greater phasic increases in systolic blood pressure, anger to greater phasic increases in diastolic blood pressure, and fear to vasoconstriction – the skin flushes.

- Progress in describing these unique responses is slow because of the difficulty of eliciting one single emotion and measuring its accompanying processes (Thompson, 1988).

- If the same site in the brain is stimulated at different times, different emotions can be produced.

- Hormonal levels influence the intensity of an emotional response.

- The physiological responses to emotion can result in related disorders, such as headaches, stomach pain, blushing, sweating, muscular tightness and diarrhoea.

- Physiological disorders are only partially connected to a conscious awareness of one's emotional state.

If we accept these possible effects it suggests that pupils can experience a wide range of emotional responses which may influence their performance. Stress and anxiety are just two of these complex emotions.

Stress and learning

The biologist Robert Sapolsky shows that while mild transient stress enhances declarative or factual learning, prolonged or severe stress disrupts it (Sapolsky, 2004). In his highly entertaining and informative writing, he shows that stress in the animal kingdom is about short-term crises; for example, the zebra running for its life while being chased by a lioness, a scenario for which both creatures are superbly equipped. He demonstrates that the brain is designed to seek homeostasis (or internal consistency), and while animals deal with events on the basis of immediate experience, humans create extra stress from anticipated events which may or may not come into being. He reduces this to two simple propositions.

- The body has a surprisingly similar set of responses to a broad array of stressors.

- If stressors go on for too long, they can make you sick.

He explains that zebras worry only about acute physical crises and dangers, where humans are able to create stress from any of their thoughts – hence the title of his celebrated book: *Why Zebras Don't Get Ulcers!*

Anxiety is a real pressure for some pupils. The causes for it may well lie outside school, or in their peer relationships. A report in 2000 from the National Society for the Prevention of Cruelty to Children (NSPCC) shows that it is a reality for one third of pupils aged 11–16, who responded they were always worried about something. High on the list of concerns is exams, with 82 per cent anxious about these. Having no one to talk their problems over with is also an issue for almost half of young people, while one in five says that they don't want to tell anyone about their problems as they don't want them to worry. When asked what would make them talk to someone about their worries, they said they valued being listened to and believed.

If we accept the evidence earlier in this chapter showing that the emotions are powerful in shaping the whole of our growth and development, including the brain, then the emotions should have higher status in the process of education at all stages. If eight out of ten secondary pupils are worried about exams, then it should be an explicit part of the curriculum to acknowledge and deal with such a concern, as it has a bearing on the whole of their lives.

 Point for reflection

What kinds of responses already exist in the curriculum, and what more could be added to acknowledge and deal with examination and other worries?

One more example here may help to make this clear. In 1983, a team of researchers from the Erasmus Medical Centre in Rotterdam gave checklists to 1,580 pupils as part of a long-term population study. They were aged between four and seventeen years old when they were first assessed and this was before Ecstasy began to be used as a recreational drug in the Netherlands. The researchers used sensitive research, based on questionnaires, to discover if the children had any of the 120 emotional or behavioural problems listed. The participants were followed up in 1997, when they were aged between eighteen and thirty-three years old. It was found that those who had signs of anxiety or depression in 1983 showed an increased risk of starting to use Ecstasy. The researchers noted that long-term use of the drug had previously been found to lead to an increased risk of depressive symptoms. The professor who led the study said that their findings did indeed show a link between childhood anxiety and later Ecstasy use (BBC News, 2006). Ecstasy has a chemical structure similar to the stimulant methamphetamine. It causes damage to serotonin which itself plays a role in regulating mood, memory, sleep and appetite and there are other symptoms of a more severe kind, including liver damage. (The issue of students understanding the impact of substances on the brain is dealt with in Chapter 6.)

We now continue with the theme of the emotions as part of the curriculum.

Naming the elephant

An interesting and elegant metaphor comes from Watkins and his colleagues (2007) which is highly relevant at this point. A group of people are talking in a room where there is also an elephant – but no-one mentions it. The elephant that is not named represents fear and, as the researchers note, it ought to be named so that something can be done about it. This metaphor is true of the emotions in general: the influence they have on many aspects of our lives, and on learning in particular, often goes unacknowledged.

There are many schools and support organisations which are happy to allow the emotions to permeate the whole curriculum. Imaginative work through the arts, particularly dance and drama, is effectively used as a vehicle to enable pupils to express their feelings more fully. One example of such an organisation is Antidote, whose aim is to support the development of emotional literacy. One of their most successful projects works through philosophical enquiry where issues are taken as they emerge, rather than just talking about feelings in general. It is based on a view of learning where pupils feel capable and supported to do their best:

> They are listened to and they are free to say what they think and feel, they are safe because it is acknowledged that feelings have an impact upon what they say, think and do. (www.antidote.org.uk)

Another organisation which is using recent brain research to develop a tool for extending their work in dealing with profound levels of feeling is Kids Company. They aim to provide children and young people with care and better opportunities in life. Using neurobiological evidence, they are seeking via neuro-imaging to discover more about the role of the reticular activating system in post-traumatic stress disorder (www.kidsco.org.uk).

Earlier in this chapter, three US psychiatrists were pleading for less emphasis on cognition and more on our understanding of the emotions. They cited Einstein who urged that:

> We should take care not to make the intellect our god; it has, of course, powerful muscles, but no personality. It cannot lead; it can only serve. (Amini et al., 2000)

It does seem from the evidence that the place of the emotions in the curriculum needs serious reconsideration. Greenspan states this argument strongly in his work describing the growth of the mind:

> We can no longer afford to ignore the emotional origins of intelligence. Theories of, say, cognitive versus emotional intelligence, however helpful in emphasising the importance of emotion, unfortunately leave us with a conception of human nature that separates two of our most important capacities. (Greenspan, 1997)

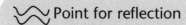Point for reflection

How can you begin to take into account your students' emotions in order to improve their performance?

The emotions and learning – from infancy to school

We saw earlier that there is a sea change taking place in our understanding of the world of the developing infant, and there are similar changes taking place now in our understanding of the earliest stages of learning. A combination of brain scanning techniques, careful observation and imaginative testing has shown important differences in children that are apparent as they enter school, in terms of their potential to take advantage of the educational experiences offered to them.

The first and in some ways the most important shift is that we can see more clearly how crucial the role of the parent or caregiver is. Perhaps for the first time, we can acknowledge that parents are the primary or main teachers. The major sources of evidence to support these and other shifts in our understanding of the capabilities of young children are drawn from the recent work of Posner and Rothbart (2007) and the many neuroscientists and researchers whose work they cite. They make the radical suggestion that education should begin in infancy and involve a continuous co-operative enterprise between home and school in shaping the neural networks involved with school subjects. A parental knowledge of what is happening in the brains of their children can serve as the basis for enlisting a new level of involvement.

Complementing notions of intelligence with other abilities

Another major departure in the Posner and Rothbart study is the move away from notions of intelligence as a defining feature of competence to considering instead children's temperaments with regard to learning. They define temperament here as 'individual differences in reactivity and self regulation, as observed within children's emotions, motor activity and attention' (Posner and Rothbart, 2007). (Note that some of this literature contains new phrases and descriptions which are not easy to understand at first.)

One of the important characteristics of early years' development that emerged in the study is called 'effortful control'. This attribute is connected to the neural network which underpins 'executive attention', and in this context it is defined as 'the ability to inhibit a dominant response to perform a subdominant response'. It is correlated with the ability to resolve conflict in tasks, and requires an ability to focus on the main events, rule out other possibilities and to delay gratification. 'Executive attention' is important for explicit learning and involves the ability to bring to mind material previously encountered. It is of great importance in learning the specific skills that are required in schools and that are a prerequisite for school exams. High effortful control, Posner and Rothbart note later, is also an indicator of 'strong empathy with others'.

Inevitably, there is a powerful emotional dimension to these characteristics of temperament and effortful control. The data Posner and Rothbart use to identify these connections include the rate of blood flow to given areas and other key neuro-imaging information. These data suggest a close interaction between cognitive and emotional regulation. For example, it seems likely that:

> strong negative emotions may inhibit the processing of cognitive information, whereas strong positive emotions may have the opposite effect.

What is significant here in terms of learning is the discovery that temperament and effortful control are essential to each child's emotional, social and cognitive development at school.

Three dimensions of the emotions and learning

There are three other factors which have a bearing on the emotional aspects of learning. The first relates to the goals which the pupils are striving to achieve (see Watkins and Lodge (2007) for an explanation of the dynamics of learning and performance). Goals are generally defined as being either for intrinsic mastery and task involvement, or for performance and ego-involvement. Substantial research suggests that children are more likely to achieve when the goals they are directed towards are meaningful and challenging outcomes and not concerned only with external rewards and social comparison (Pintrich, 1993). In other words, the children will achieve because they are interested in the task and learning for its own sake, rather than 'doing work' to please the teacher. The value and importance of appropriate goals are well put by Covington:

> Ultimately it is the value and meaning of what is learned – more particularly, the sense of satisfaction arising from enhanced understanding – rather than accumulating knowledge for the sake of power or prestige that will ultimately determine whether the will to learning is maintained. (Covington, 1999)

The second and equally important factor comes from the work of Carol Dweck. In her research she found that those children who see intelligence as a fixed entity, and therefore that they are either smart or dumb, are disadvantaged when compared to those who have a more flexible view. The latter group sees that intelligence is open to change and that application is an important factor. Children as young as three and a half can have a negative view of their learning abilities, or, as Dweck (2000) puts it, 'a negative self entity'.

The third factor is the ability to get on with people. Although this is not often alluded to as a dimension related to attainment, it most certainly is an important empirical factor for teachers. Adaptation to school involves social interaction with teachers, classmates and other adults, and the ability to interpret the emotional states of others is important for successful social action (Posner and Rothbart, 2007).

There are other dimensions of the emotions that influence learning, including the power of fear that Posner and Robart refer to. However, the key point about their still emerging and important work is that it is based directly on evidence about the brain. Their research is introducing fresh perspectives and vocabulary, including self-regulation, temperament and effortful control, which build on the studies of learning in infancy and the relationship between caregiver and child that we have seen earlier in this chapter. They provide a vital missing connection between what happens in the earliest stages of life and the beginnings of school. The emotional development of the child is central here, and should be a major concern for all who are involved with the care and education of our children.

 Point for reflection

Goals with real meaning for pupils, their views of their intelligence and their ability to get on with each other are three aspects of success in school. How do you plan to include these as and when you can?

Movement, touch and emotion

This is a very sensitive issue, but one that is key to the development of a full emotional life. As we saw earlier in this chapter, the term 'emotion' is derived from the Latin *movere* – to move. Emotion describes an outward movement which is a way of communicating and demonstrating our most important internal states and needs. John Ratey (2001) argues that

> the motor and emotional systems probably evolved concurrently in primates.

He then explains that geographically the motor and emotional systems are right beside each other in the brain. The limbic system is wrapped around the movement system, so there is some degree of interconnection. Young children have a natural propensity for movement and they often express their feelings through it. In fact, it is difficult at any age to express a powerful emotion without some movement. Movement connects with other facets of life and learning as well, as Carla Hannaford illustrates here:

> As children encounter new information, they will move to embody it on all their muscles and senses. Allow yourself to be guided on a walk with a three year old child. When they come to something new, they will actually move their bodies to conform to the physical configuration of the new object. Movement facilitates the entrainment process in understanding relationships physically. (Hannaford, 1995)

Hannaford also explains that children who are allowed to express emotions naturally and responsibly are better able to use them constructively or creatively throughout life. The whole area of the curriculum for young children is under threat, if we are unable to see the vital importance of movement and imaginative play. There is huge pressure from higher up the age range to narrow downwards and formalise too soon. A recent Ofsted survey of 144 early years settings noted that:

> Achievement was lower in imaginative play because practitioners gave it too little attention. (Ofsted, 2007)

There was some criticism in this same report of speaking and listening skills, which are closely connected with the quality of and opportunity for direct experience (as noted in the previous chapter). If we are to take the notion of learning for life seriously, then movement should be at the centre of the curriculum and for all ages.

The importance of touch in the lives of children

This is a problematic issue. Whenever I work with early years staff, I am asked the same question over and over: 'What about touching children?' The question reflects not only a genuine professional anxiety, but also a serious doubt in our society about the value and place of touching. It is perhaps surprising that the evidence about touch for young children in so many studies is unequivocal: it is essential to growth. We possess an instinct both to touch and be touched that is fundamental to human development. Ratey here makes clear the significance of touch for the development of the brain:

> Touch is far more than a sensory apparatus. Our sense of touch affects the development and expansion of our brains, well into adulthood. It is a key component in growing, learning, communicating and living. A baby's touch is a significant factor in the development of certain areas of the brain ... When you watch a baby touch, you are watching the development of intelligence in his or her cortex. (Ratey, 2001)

If you watch a newborn baby in the early weeks of its life, you will certainly notice how important touch is. A classic study by Tiffany Field and colleagues which demonstrates the significance of this is described by Sapolsky:

> Studying premature infants in neonatal wards, they noted that the premature kids, while pampered and fretted over, were hardly ever touched. So Field and crew went in and started touching them for

fifteen minute periods, three times a day, stroking their bodies and moving their limbs. It worked wonders. The kids grew nearly fifty per cent faster, were more active and alert, matured faster behaviourally and were released from hospital nearly a week earlier than the premature infants who weren't touched. Months later they were still doing better than the infants who hadn't been touched. (Sapolsky, 2004)

An extreme example of this profound need for touch and physical contact is evident from the work of medical school researcher Mary Carlson referred to earlier, who in the 1990s visited the overcrowded orphanages of Romania. She found hundreds of swaddled babies in cribs who were never touched, not even during feeding times. Some of the babies had lived that way for nearly two years. Her studies showed that the babies were stunted in growth, acted at about half their age and had abnormal levels of the stress-fighting hormone cortisol, compared with babies who had been raised in homes nearby (Ratey, 2001).

 Point for reflection

The evidence clearly shows the value and importance of touch for children, but how can we manage this in an institution, with regard to their safety and wellbeing?

Child rearing practices differ, and there are approaches current in Britain that may not be in the best interests of the child. For example, some babies are being deprived of their mother's touch because of the excessive use of pushchairs and detachable car seats rather than slings. Babies in a sling can sense their mother's heartbeat, hear her voice and generally participate when awake by seeing the world around them. Not so the infant in the Boadicean chariot, out of sight and it seems almost out of mind, for the adult's convenience. There is some good news though, with a resurgence in baby massage as noted by the Director of the Touch Research Institute at the Miami School of Medicine. Dr Clark noted the many benefits of massage, among them the stimulation of activity in the vagus nerve – one of the 12 cranial nerves which help to relax the central nervous system (see the *Telegraph*, news.co.uk, 15 September 2004).

It is clear that children thrive on touch and physical contact. Most importantly though, as Lise Eliot notes in her comprehensive work on early intelligence:

Because touch more than any other sense, has such ready access to young babies' brains, it offers the best possible opportunity, and one of the easiest, for moulding their emotional and mental well being. (Eliot, 2001)

We have to search for an answer to the question at the beginning of this section as to how adults working with young children should use touch. Of course this has to be negotiated with parents at the school level, and at the very least it should be discussed.

 Point for reflection

Given the substantial and varied evidence in this chapter about the importance of parents, how would you or do you already acknowledge their role as educators?

Pupils' feelings about their experience of life and learning in school

Pupils spend a lot of their young lives in school, but there is little opportunity for them to express their feelings about what they enjoy, what goes well and what creates problems for them both as individual personalities and as learners. This is in spite of the evidence presented earlier in this chapter illustrating how powerful the emotions are in helping or frustrating the achievement of our goals. Here we reflect on responses from pupils in two surveys: the first was conducted in one primary school and the second, much larger one, in eight others. In the questionnaires they were given, many answers were multiple-choice, but for some questions pupils were given the opportunity to produce their own answers. The questions covered a range of school experiences, and some of these gave pupils the opportunity to comment on their feelings.

The responses of 300 children in one London primary school, highlighted the issue of friendship. When asked 'What makes you feel happy in your class?' almost half of pupils chose the answer 'My friends'. This may not be very surprising, but it does imply that for many pupils the social aspects of being in school are very important. Similarly, in answer to the question 'What makes you feel unhappy in your class?' about a third chose the answer 'Some people', indicating a strong social element in many pupils' emotional state in school. Where the issue becomes really crucial with regard to learning is in answering the question 'What stops you from working better?' In this case nearly half said 'Talking to my friends'. In the second study of eight schools, with almost 2000 pupils involved, there was a similar response to this same question. It raises an important issue for discussion with pupils since, assuming the response is accurate, informal talking is seriously inhibiting the learning of many of them. Discussion prompted by this information could focus on ways to enable social conversation with friends that does not have a negative impact on learning, and perhaps over time, on pupils' chances of achieving what they expect to gain from school. A discussion of this kind acknowledges that the social dimension of school is a reality, but that the primary purpose is learning.

Nearly a third of pupils in the larger study responded to the question 'What makes you unhappy in class?' with the answer 'People being unkind to me'. This suggests an important area for exploration that could be beneficial in helping some pupils to gain more from their school experience.

 Point for reflection

Is there a point at which you could ask your students/pupils about what makes them unhappy in class or school and what responses they can suggest for improvement?

One school in the larger survey chose to explore some of the pupils' feelings about particular aspects of life in school. The question was asked 'When do you feel nervous at school?' Very few said they never felt nervous, and most said they felt anxious about some aspects of lessons some of the time, but a fairly large minority admitted to being very nervous most of the time, particularly about tests. They worried about them at all stages – in preparation, during the tests and afterwards while waiting for the results. There should be time set aside for pupils to talk about their feelings in relation to tests, both in order to improve their attainment and to understand how their emotions influence their performance.

When asked 'If you do not understand what the teacher is asking, how do you feel?' nearly half the children expressed negative emotions such as anxiety, or being scared to ask for help in case the teacher told them off for not listening. There is no implicit criticism of teachers here, and this could reflect any classroom. However, few teachers would want this level of misunderstanding so it does suggest that pupils should have more opportunity to say what they are thinking – and particularly what they are feeling.

Learning to control the emotions

There is a further dimension of brain research which shows possibilities for the future. Until recently the 'set point' theory of emotional mood was largely accepted. According to this, people have an inborn 'set point' for mood, which is rather like a default setting on a computer. The set point – your basic level of happiness or sadness – returns, even if you experience great happiness or grief (Ratey, 2001). Now there is new evidence to challenge this idea from a unique study involving eight experienced Buddhist meditators, and eight non-meditators as a control group. This work is reported more fully in the final chapter, but it is relevant to note an interesting finding here.

When focusing on activating the pre-frontal cortex which has connections with the amygdala, the experimental group was able to reduce activation in this area, and to demonstrate that fear can be modulated with mental training (Begley, 2007). Of course, the individuals in the experimental group were trained meditators, but nevertheless, the researchers concluded that:

> the plasticity of the brain's emotional circuits is the means by which mental training can bring about enduring physical changes in the brain and hence in one's mental and emotional state. (Begley, 2007)

We may be a long way from this work becoming an actuality, but it does suggest that discussing emotional states for learning and well-being is potentially a future part of the curriculum.

Conclusion

In this chapter I have attempted to show how the emotions are central to learning and brain growth, and how they are best nurtured in a loving relationship, hopefully leading to intellectual curiosity and mastery. I have therefore suggested that the role of parents needs more status as part of the education process, and that the curriculum needs to acknowledge the power and importance of the emotions for learning. Finally, I have shown how the thoughts and feelings of pupils about the quality of life and learning in school can provide teachers with vital information about their learning.

If you wish to follow through with some of the themes in this chapter, you will find the following books particularly helpful.

Descartes' Error: Emotion Reason and the Human Brain – Damasio (1994)

Antonio Damasio is not only a world-renowned neurologist, he is also an elegant writer who is able to explain complex ideas to the lay person. He presents a clear view of how reason and emotions interact to produce our decisions and plans for action. He is the first major neuroscientist to show unequivocally that the emotions are part of cognition. This is obviously of great importance for educators.

Why Love Matters: How Affection Shapes a Baby's Brain – Gerhardt (2004)

Sue Gerhardt is a practising psychotherapist and she explains why love is essential to brain development in the early years. It is a humane and wise work that examines how important loving relationships shape our capacities to be human.

A General Theory of Love – Amini et al. (2000)

The authors, (three American psychiatrists), challenge the social patterns that have emerged in American society through insights from many fields, particularly neuroscience. They present a critique of the way in which children are brought up and educated. They also claim that who we are and who we become depend in large part upon whom we love. They also show that in a relationship, one mind revises another and that one heart changes its partner. It is both challenging and beautifully written.

Here are some of the ways in which the emotions have implications for learning from the evidence in this chapter:

- Motivation is the connecting force between the emotions and action.

- The emotions are fundamental to all communication.

- The emotions are central to both brain growth and learning.

- The governing function that promotes healthy brain development and physical and emotional development is unconditional love.

- In our close relationships, we have a significant impact on the physiology of others.

- The development of learning grows from an understanding of interdependence as well as the desire for independence.

- 'The unimpeachable fact' is that love matters enormously in the life of a child.

- The Nun Study shows the connection between longevity and the ability to express emotions.

- Anxiety and stress can have effects upon performance in school.

- A disregard or contempt for the emotions leads to feral behaviour and in some cases to violence.

- The beginnings of our life set the stage for every aspect of our internal and external functions throughout the whole of life.

- Nine months before birth and nine months afterwards form the first stage of dependent development.

- Both the relationship and the gaze between mother and infant are of great importance.

- The second stage is the act of separation which begins towards the end of the first year and continues during the second year.

- Body and brain need to be seen as an integrated system.

- There are vital connections between movement and emotion, hence the value of play, music and movement, drama, physical education and games.

- Touch is important for physical and emotional growth, and it has high status in some cultures.

- Recent research points to three factors for success in school: these are temperament, effortful control and the ability to get on with others.

Next we will consider the third side of the triangle – how memory is established and what helps its development.

5

Memory, the brain and learning

> We are not who we are simply because we think. We are who we are because we can remember what we have thought about. (Squire, 2000)

In this chapter, we examine what brain research can tell us about the nature and functioning of memory. We see that the functions of attention, emotion and memory are three sides of a triangle which interconnect and support each other and they are to a large extent interdependent. We will also consider the various aspects of memory that influence children in school. Here you will learn more about:

- how our earliest memories are autobiographical and essential to the development of our self-concept;

- how self-knowledge is also essential for the development of our self-concept, and mainly created from what we learn implicitly from what is happening around us;

- how memory influences our self-image as a learner and therefore has an influence upon our attainment;

- how working memory is also essential for our attainment and for our survival;

- how there are several typologies for memory, but the most common is the division into procedural memory (which is knowing how to do things like riding a bicycle) and declarative memory (which is the recall of facts);

y there is research evidence which illustrates the difference
ween the memory strategies of expert and novices;

- how there is also evidence that sleep is important for remembering, although it is not conclusive, except with procedural memory;

- how in our surveys with pupils, we found that most pupils had strategies for memory, but some were more effective than others;

- how we consider strategies for helping pupils to improve their ability to remember.

Why memory is important for learning

Memory has been the focus of many research studies, and evidence from these indicates that it serves multiple purposes in our lives and our learning. A major function of memory is described here:

> Memory defines who we are and shapes the way we act more closely than any other single aspect of our personhood. (Rose, 1992)

So says Steven Rose, the well known author and neuroscientist. He goes on to discuss the paradox at the heart of the issue of memory that can't be explained. During a human lifetime, every molecule of the body is replaced many times over. Cells die and others take their place, and the connections between them are broken innumerable times. And yet, despite this endless flux, our memories remain, albeit as we shall see, not always indelibly inscribed.

Leaving this fascinating biological conundrum to one side for now, it becomes clear that the key researchers in the field of memory studies ascribe a more powerful function to memory than just the acquiring and storing of facts. Memory is the very understanding of the self – what it means to be you! To use memory effectively and creatively in school for learning, we need to understand both its origins and its multiple purposes in our lives.

Emotions and memory

Emotions can profoundly affect memory and learning in a variety of ways. Damasio explains:

The process of learning and recalling emotionally competent events is different with conscious feelings from what it would be without feelings. Some feelings optimize learning and recall. Other feelings, extremely painful feelings in particular, perturb learning and protectively suppress recall. In general, memory of the felt situation promotes, consciously or not, the avoidance of events associated with negative feelings and the seeking of situations that may cause positive feelings. (Damasio, 2003)

In other words, our memories are selective and often leave out painful events.

Jonathan Turner notes that memory requires an emotional component, and for an evolutionary reason. He explains that not all memories which guide our thoughts and actions are conscious. Selection enhanced the fitness of primitive mammals to remember in different ways. Thus some memories were made under the influence of bodily responses that store emotional memories outside the purview of the neo-cortex. As he puts it:

Some individuals are often at a loss cognitively to understand why they make certain decisions, or behave in certain ways. (Turner, 2000)

Noticing is an integral part of remembering

Steve Mithen makes another connection with our evolutionary past in his observations of the behaviour of chimpanzees in the West African Tai forest. These animals regularly carry stones to particular places in the forest, and use them as hammers and anvils to break up nuts for feeding. From their observations and measurements of these activities, the researchers concluded that the chimps rely on noticing and remembering sufficient information about the environment to guide them on their daily journey.

Mithen's work demonstrates further the significance of attention that we saw in Chapter 3, and connects attention and memory to the notion of intentionality or purpose (Mithen, 1996). Walter Freeman provides a rationale for showing how attention, emotion and memory interact through the power of intention. He proposes a simple model where an action requires emotion (or drive), attention (or noticing), and some recall of previous experience. Each of these elements is apparent in the above story of the chimps. Thus memory completes the third side of the triangle, with attention and emotion on the other two sides.

emotion, attention, memory

iographical memory and the sense of self

ographical memory – each individual's unique internalised history – does not begin to develop until the cognitive self is established. This, according to Mark Howe and colleagues (himself an expert in the development of memory in young children), happens towards the end of the second year of life, but others from the sociolinguistic tradition hold that autobiographical memory follows a child's ability to establish a personal life story in memory. This, they say, may not occur until the pre-school years, since autobiographical memory requires a certain level of linguistic and narrative competence (Howe et al., 2003). No doubt the true picture is somewhere between the two, but the fact is that the developing child's experience of memory is largely related to the narrative of events in their day-to-day life, and that of the adults they live with.

The question of the nature of memory in young children is of interest here. Rose refers to this as in some cases 'eidetic' (Rose, 1992). It resembles photographic memory with vivid visual images in accurate detail, and is quite different from adult memory:

> Many if not all young children apparently do normally see and remember eidetically, but this capacity is lost to most as they grow up.

The connection between attention and the development of short-term memory has been investigated by researchers from the University of Iowa. Their work shows that infants at ten months of age can encode items into the short-term memory, which is crucial for their learning about the world around them (Sheehy, 2005). They emphasise that infant short-term memory is mediated by and reliant upon 'relatively well developed attention mechanisms', and that this ability does not appear to be evident in younger infants.

A sense of self

While infants are learning how to observe, categorise and remember objects and activities in the world around them, they are also learning about themselves. This personal knowledge is even more important in terms of making the choices and decisions that will ultimately lead to the personality of the individual. Klein et al. (2004) provide a matrix of three essential capabilities needed in order to experience memory as autobiographical self-knowledge:

1 a capacity for self-reflection (the ability to reflect on one's own mental states);

2 a sense of personal agency or ownership (the belief that one is the cause of one's thoughts and actions);

3 the ability to think about time, as an unfolding of personal happenings centred about the self.

Klein and his colleagues believe that our knowledge of self is very much tied up with the story of our experience and how that makes us who we are.

 Point for reflection

A key part of the curriculum for young children is to use their previous experience as an essential tool for developing memory. How much of this is this done in your school or setting?

Greenspan further claims that:

If all goes well, growing children will be able to create in childhood a strong self-image consisting of pictures, words, feelings and other remembered sensations. (Greenspan, 1997)

In a more recent work, he identifies why this is so essential for our future lives:

Without a sense of self, there is no stable internal compass or frame of reference upon which to compare, contrast, or make judgements. It is not by chance that this sense of self becomes more organized and complex as the capacity for reflective thinking and making judgements about one's own behaviour and thoughts becomes apparent. (Greenspan, 2004)

Damasio sees the self as based on personal memory:

The autobiographical self depends on systematized memories of situations in which core consciousness was involved in the knowing of the most invariant characteristics of an organism's life – who you were born to, where, when, your likes and dislikes, the way you usually react to a problem or a conflict, your name and so on. (Damasio, 1999)

sence then, it is the composite of our memories that makes us
uely who we are. It depends on the sum of our implicit and
explicit memories, the area to which we turn next.

Implicit and explicit memories

Where these aspects of childhood memory can have a bearing on
pupils' achievement in school is with the notion of implicit memory.
This is where we absorb information without being aware of it, since
the brain is able to process and store information without us knowing
about it. It is important to note that 'implicit knowledge can remain
hidden' (Blakemore and Frith, 2005). Self-knowledge is profoundly
important in the life path of each individual, yet the powerful learning it requires is often implicit and unseen.

The Nobel prize winner Eric Kandel points out that:

> Implicit memory is not a single memory system, but a collection of
> processes involving several brain systems that lie deep within the cere-
> bral cortex. (Kandel, 2006)

Implicit memory is made up from events and experiences in our
early environment, and reflects how we are thought of and spoken
to, and what happens in our relationships. In contrast, explicit memory encodes factual knowledge like names, faces and events – the
kind of things we need to remember consciously.

Implicit memory can have an impact on our learning as it contains
our attitudes to others and ourselves. An example of this is described
in Carol Dweck's work (Dweck, 2000). Pupils' views of their own
intelligence are critical for attainment, and she shows how those
views may be formed unconsciously through the way parents react
to their behaviour. She observed children role-playing harsh criticism
and punishment from a parent, and believes that this shows they felt
deeply judged by their own parents – an example of the negative
potential of implicit memory where some children carry the burden
of others' poor expectations. Dweck shows how taking an incremental approach – where intelligence is regarded as open to change – can
be effective in helping children to move from a negative to a positive
self-image, and so to improved achievement. Hers is perhaps the first
major work to attempt to embrace the duality for learners of their
implicit and explicit memories. As the biologist Zull explains:

This distinction between explicit and implicit memory has many implications for a teacher. Behaviours, beliefs and feelings can all be stored in
implicit memory, so when we want someone to learn, we must watch for
these as well as for what they remember explicitly. (Zull, 2002)

Recent research from Carol Dweck (2000) has found evidence that
students who believe that intelligence is plastic or incremental, and
that it can be developed, perform better. Although all the students
began the study with equivalent achievement levels in mathematics,
over a two-year period those who believed that intelligence was mal-
leable did better than those who believed their intelligence was fixed.
Another study found that when students who had declining maths
grades were taught that intelligence could be increased, they reversed
their decline and showed significantly higher maths grades than others
who weren't given this information (Blackwell, 2007).

 Point for reflection

> Pupils' views of their intelligence are often influenced by their
> implicit memories. Choose a few of your students and ask them for
> their views of their intelligence and performance and see if these
> match your perceptions. What kinds of evidence are they using for
> their self-judgements?

Memory then is fundamental to our repertoire of survival strategies
and to the learning process, and is closely linked with the emotions
and attention. We now move on to consider the act of remembering.

The act of remembering

An essential feature of memory is that it doesn't exist in a single centre in the brain. Ratey notes that 'there is no single centre for vision,
language, emotion, behaviour ... or memory' (Ratey, 2001). The act
of calling to mind an object requires bringing together the different
kinds of information that are spread across various cortical sites, and
reassembling the information into a coherent whole (Squire, 2000).

Retrieval cues
Retrieval cues are stimuli or thoughts that instigate the transfer of
long-term memory into working memory (Western, 1999). They are

al for retrieving coded information from different parts of the
Two of the major researchers into memory, Endel Tulving and
Shacter, emphasise the role of retrieval cues in remembering,
along with other researchers such as Kandel and Squire. There is
common agreement that:

> To be effective, retrieval instructions or cues must be able to revivify
> the memory, and the most effective retrieval cues are those that
> awaken the best encoded aspects of the event that you are trying to
> remember. (Squire, 2000)

This is important for learning, as encoding or embedding influences
the extent of neuronal change in the brain. To illustrate how this
may happen, Squire and Kendal describe a simple experiment in
which two groups of volunteers study the same list of 12 words.
Group A is asked to determine the number of letters in each word
that are formed by straight lines (e.g., F, V and H), while Group B is
asked to process the meaning of each word and to rate on a scale of
one to five how much they liked each word. A short time later, both
groups write down as many words as they can remember. The results
are dramatic and consistent: those who process meaning remember
two to three times as many words as those that focus on the shapes
of the letters. This may seem self-evident, but the experiment very
clearly illustrates a vital point about learning:

> We remember better the more fully we process new subject matter.
> (Squire, 2000)

(Processing in this case means attending to the meaning.)

Furthermore memory is better:

- the more we have a powerful purpose for study;

- the more we enjoy what we are studying;

- the more we can bring the full breadth of our personality to the
  task. (Squire, 2000)

We will look at successful strategies for remembering in the final section of this chapter, through the study of an outstanding practitioner
of memory techniques. First we turn to working memory, which is so
vital to our ability to function in daily life.

Working memory

There is no overall consensus among theorists on the ways to classify memory, but one area of agreement is the distinction between short- and long-term memory. Short-term memory is now more generally known as working memory, as it registers what we need to know to function in the present. Ratey describes it as:

> the mental glue that holds connections together, as we think a thought or enact a process from beginning to end. (Ratey, 2001)

Long-term memory is encoded and put into more permanent storage in the brain, requiring the growth of new synaptic connections.

Working memory is an essential part of what it is to be human. It enables us to act in particular ways and to make choices and decisions from minute to minute. Perhaps its importance is seen most clearly when it is impaired, as for instance in patients with Alzheimer's who are unable to function independently because of the loss of their working memory. Current evidence shows that a working memory system starts to develop in infants between six and twelve months and shows protracted development throughout childhood (Johnson, 2005). Kandel (2006) points out that the main difference between long-term and working memory is time-related: working memory operates over minutes or perhaps hours, while long-term memory spans days to years.

Pupils in school will retain the task that they have been given in their working memory, while they process the requirements of the task and carry it out. Holding three or four task components in the memory is easy for some pupils, but problematic for others, and those for whom it is a particular difficulty may need additional help to develop their working memory. This, along with practice in attention, forms a set of sub-skills that are essential for learning, and in some cases they need to be taught discretely.

 Point for reflection

Are there any of your students who have difficulty with holding information in their working memory, particularly when they have to remember verbal instructions for a task? If so, what strategies might be helpful for them?

Training to improve working memory

Recent studies suggest that working memory can be improved with training, where previously it had been thought to be fixed. Torkel Klingberg carried out two experiments with healthy adult human subjects who practised working memory tasks for five weeks. He measured brain activity with Functional Resonance Magnetic Imaging (fMRI) before, during and after the training, and found that after the training, brain activity that was related to working memory increased in the middle frontal gyrus and superior and inferior parietal cortices. The changes in cortical activity could be evidence of 'training-induced plasticity in the neural systems that underlie working memory' – in other words, working memory can be improved with training (Klingberg, 2004).

It seems clear from other studies that the ability to hold more than one variable in the mind is an essential part of what we understand as intelligence. Consequently, improving or augmenting the brain's working memory is likely to have a beneficial effect on attainment.

Ambiguity and real-life situations

Elkhonon Goldberg, in his influential work on the frontal lobes, identifies another dimension to problem solving that involves memory. He notes the paradoxical situation whereby in school we are commonly given problems where there is only one answer. This is in contrast with real life situations where the problems are inherently ambiguous and may have multiple solutions. He explains it thus:

> Finding solutions for deterministic situations is often accomplished algorithmically. It is increasingly delegated to various devices, calculators, computers and directories of all kinds. However, making choices in the absence of inherently correct solutions remains, at least for now, a uniquely human territory. In a sense, the freedom of choice is possible only when ambiguity is present. (Goldberg, 2001)

Goldberg is suggesting that the cognitive processes involved in resolving ambiguous situations are very different from those involved in solving strictly right or wrong contexts. Finding real-life situations where pupils have to make choices and resolve ambiguities is important training for the real world that they actually have to deal with.

Point for reflection

Are there any curriculum areas where you feel your students could benefit from dealing with ambiguous situations, perhaps that are to closer real-life experience?

As well as dealing with ambiguity, students need to have some understanding of meta-memory – that is, knowledge of the strengths and weaknesses of one's own memory. For example, studies of human amnesia show that the working memory can be transposed into long-term memory within as little a time as 60 seconds. The memory is quickly reorganised, and it is this reorganised subjective and interpreted information that is later retrieved for use. An important implication of this research is that we can never describe in exact detail what was actually presented to us, for as soon as we experience something, we immediately interpret and rewire it (Ratey, 2001). This is easy to demonstrate to pupils in the classroom by arranging a short dramatic event which they are asked to observe and then asking them to recall it a little later. Invariably, each student will have a different interpretation of what they have seen.

Procedural memory

Implicit memory

Procedural memory (also known as non-declarative memory) is knowing how to do things. Automatically storing processes for routine actions is the first function of memory to develop in the early stages of brain growth. For infants, learning how to grasp things, for instance, is a vital step forwards to gaining personal control and mastery. Greenspan cites evidence suggesting that:

> Procedural or implicit memory, which involves the sub-symbolic emotional systems, functions very shortly after birth, while declarative or explicit memory which involves symbolic cortical processes and conscious awareness, gradually starts operating by four years of age. (Greenspan, 2004)

Many procedural memories are acquired through imitation. This is a very natural process for infants and involves mirror neurons (as we saw in Chapter 3).

Point for reflection

To help pupils to understand their unconscious memory, ask them to describe to a friend a relatively simple process like cutting paper with scissors. Get them to notice how important gesture can be for this process.

An example of procedural memory in operation with adults is driving a car. Learning to co-ordinate several processes – such as braking, changing gear and indicating to turn – is very demanding. Once mastered, however, the processes quickly become automatic. I sometimes ask groups I am working with how many of them can actually remember driving themselves there, and I usually find that a significant number of them have no recollection at all of their recent journey. Driving is so automatic for them that it has become unconscious. Procedural functions such as riding a bicycle may also become unconscious to the point that it is difficult for someone who can do it to describe the series of actions required to someone who can't. Bruner called these processes of know-how 'a memory without record' (Squire, 2000).

Declarative memory

Eric Kandel (2006) reminds us that:

> memory enables us to solve the problems we confront in everyday life by marshalling several facts at once, an ability that is vital to problem-solving.

This is what we normally think of as memory – our memory for facts, ideas, events and information that can be brought to conscious recollection as a verbal proposition or a visual image. It is known as declarative memory. Kandel and Squire define all other memory forms as non-declarative (Squire, 2000).

Declarative memory itself has two aspects – the ability to recall a fact and the ability to recall an event, and these form two further subdivisions: episodic memory for events, and semantic memory for facts, words and rules. Episodic memory is sometimes called source memory, because it involves when and where things happen. It is hugely important in our lives for all aspects of remembering.

Episodic memory and narrative

Using narratives to help store memories was clearly demonstrated by Professor Robert Winston in the BBC television series *The Human Mind*. He interviewed an aboriginal tracker about the techniques he used to find crocodiles. The tracker explained how he made a story out of the patterns and events of the natural environment to ensure that he knew where he was. Once again, these processes involve noticing and attending in order to memorise information for survival purposes.

Kieran Egan also discusses the significance of 'storying' for humans, particularly children, as they make sense of their worlds:

> The invention of the story was a crucial stage in the discovery of the mind. What was invented was a narrative form that worked at increasing the memorability of its contents. In recognising its power and refining it through millennia, people discovered something remarkable about how the human mind works. We are a storying animal; we make sense of things commonly in story forms, ours is a largely story-shaped world. (Egan, 1988)

When considering developmental changes in memory strategies, Sara Meadows notes the stage when children begin to use narrative to help the storage and retrieval of information. She describes 'verbal elaboration' – making up a story which includes items to be remembered, such as 'the tiger in the boat is eating a bun' (Meadows, 1993). This further demonstrates then the importance for our future development of children's early experience with stories.

Rhymes, scripts and episodic memory

The importance of pre-school experience of songs and games is underlined by Iona Opie in her work with children's nursery rhymes and fairy tales. These are, she says:

> the first furnishings of the mind; the bottom-most layer of the comfortable hereditary clutter of mottoes, proverbs and half-remembered tales that we use to ornament conversations throughout our lives, knowing that they are common currency. (Iona Opie, foreword of Michael Foreman's *Nursery Rhymes*)

It seems clear that rhythm, rhyme, repetition, mnemonics and music all contribute to young children developing their memories.

The psychologist Susan Engel explains how children put their experience into sequences or 'scripts'.

> In infancy we apprehend the world as a series of routines that we represent as scripts. So, for instance, the toddler has a breakfast script, a going-to-the-park script and a bedtime script. Each of theses scripts allows the child to know what to expect in a given experience – what will come first, who will participate, and what will happen next. (Engel, 1999)

She considers that this form of remembering in episodic memory is facilitated and enhanced when adults reminisce with children about their experiences.

 Point for reflection

Notice how the use of scripts and sequences is linked to the narrative in the earliest stories we hear.

Episodic memory may be open to invention. Pat Wolfe describes the process as 'refabrication', where a memory is reconstructed with bits and pieces of the truth. As we tell our stories over and over again we add to and embellish them. Eventually the refabrication becomes the memory (Wolfe, 2001). Thus episodic memories may be vivid, but they can also be inaccurate.

Semantic memory

Semantic memory is less open to distortion than episodic as it essentially concerns facts. It includes our general knowledge of the world, the rules of disciplines such as grammar, mathematics and words, and the symbols that represent them. A key feature of semantic memory is that the remembered items are largely removed from personal time and space. If you remember the fact that $9 \times 8 = 72$ you are using semantic memory, but if you recall the room you were in or the people who were with you at the time you learnt this, you are using episodic memory.

Attention to memory

As we have seen in Chapter 3, the processes of attention are essential to intellectual growth and development. Interaction between the infant and caregiver by means of the gaze is both profound and important for the development of these processes. Further, during the first few months of life, infants are drawn to attend to novel objects by looking at them. During this period their visual acuity improves week by week, together with their ability to direct their attention, and they learn to anticipate where an object may appear (Posner and Rothbart, 2007). The development of such attention processes is both a precursor of and a necessity for memory.

Minds of their own

Posner and Rothbart note the rapid change that occurs between the ages of four months and two years in terms of attention. The four-month-old infants they observed in their research responded indiscriminately to any and all of the stimuli presented to them, but the two-year-olds reacted more purposefully – they had recall of the situation and knew what they wanted to do.

one, growing & pruning

Posner and Rothbart ascribe this major shift in behaviour to the development of the 'executive attention' system, which they believe is essential to the regulation of both emotions and cognition. They note too, that executive attention is important in explicit learning, which involves being able to recall material previously encountered. It is essential to use attention to put the memory in a form that can be brought to mind and reinstated later.

Experts and novices

The vital connection between attention and memory is further highlighted by the authors when they point to the differences between experts and novices. Expertise, they note, requires:

> being able to access material stored in the memory rapidly and automatically. (Posner and Rothbart, 2007)

The basis of expertise is the organisation of the memory system in the field of competence of the individual. Part of this structure is facilitated by understanding categories, semantic maps, imagery, reasoning and metaphor.

Expertise – ten years to mastery!

Posner and Rothbart discuss differences in the way experts and novices use their memories. They refer to work with children who are experts about dinosaurs, and adults who are experts about physics, which reveals the increased cohesiveness of their concepts in memory (Chi, 1983). The study reveals that experts, whether adult or child, tend to use the relations among things in their thinking, whereas novices deal more with the surface features of individual instances. Experts use terms such as *because* and *if*, showing relationships, whereas novices tend to produce lists of features (Posner and Rothbart, 2007). There is a distinct contrast between experts using a depth of analysis against novices using more superficial commentary.

There is a parallel here with the meteoric rise to success of the motor racing prodigy Lewis Hamilton. At present, he has taken part in nine grand prix and has achieved nine podium finishes, which means he was in the top three in each of his first races at the highest level in the sport. One member of his behind-the-scenes team is a neuroscientist, Dr Kerry Spackman, who describes two main features of Hamilton's winning abilities. The first is an ability to physically slow down the body, including using deep and slow breathing to maintain a state of calm and focused attention. The second ability derives from hours spent in a 'super simulator'. It involves the memory storage of many eventualities and possibilities. Spackman explains:

> unless you store the memories and consequences of everything you have done, you won't be able to analyse them and know what to do differently next. (Williams, 2007)

The emphasis here is on the storage and subsequent analysis of the material which is similar to the comments about the experts above.

 Point for reflection

Do your pupils want to be an expert or a master of their discipline? If so, they need to notice not only the amount of practice that is needed, but the quality of attention to subtle aspects of performance.

Another analysis of the qualities of experts occurs in the much cited work of Ericsson (2002). On the basis of his research, Ericsson concludes that the expert's brain engages differently from the amateur's. In a study he carried out at a West Berlin music academy, 'superior' students, judged by their teachers as most likely to go on to concert careers, put in an average of 24 practice hours per week; 'good' students, thought more likely to end up as teachers than performers, practised an average of only nine hours per week. By the age of twenty, the 'good' students had put in an estimated 4000 hours of practice, while the harder working future performers had notched up an estimated 10,000 hours. A similar pattern was found by Ericsson amongst superior athletes, chess players and mathematicians, and he concludes:

> For the superior performer the goal isn't just repeating the same thing again and again, but achieving higher levels of control over every aspect of their performance. That's why they don't find practice boring. Each practice session they are working on doing something better than they did the last time. (cited in Restak, 2003)

Restak (2003) believes that such high performing individuals develop advanced memory skills:

> Individuals who perform at higher levels utilize specific kinds of memory processes. They have acquired refined mental representations to maintain access to relevant information and support more extensive flexible reasoning about encountered tasks or information. Better performers are able to rapidly encode, store and manipulate information.

He analyses the experience of top golfers to explain more about how these refined processes operate in the brain:

> The expert as opposed to the amateur golfer, by mentally attending to extremely subtle aspects of his performance during practice sessions, has successfully transferred this knowledge into working memory within his frontal lobes.

This is very similar to the memory strategies used by Lewis Hamilton that we discussed earlier.

Ian Robertson, Professor of Psychology at Trinity College, Dublin, believes the evidence of improved performance for the elite has relevance for all of us. He acknowledges the value of Ericsson's estimate of ten years to achieve the highest level of expertise, but claims as well that almost any human skill can be improved with training and practice:

> Take memory for numbers, for instance, a task that is included in some of the most widely used IQ tests. The scientists studying expertise showed that students could be trained to improve substantially their ability to remember strings of numbers. (Robertson, 1999)

This evidence suggests we should be cautious about attaching too much importance to test results.

To sleep – perchance to remember?

There is growing evidence that sleep plays an important part in learning and memory, but there is as yet no universal agreement about this. The contrary view is put by Vertes and Siegel, who claim to have presented a 'wealth of data' refuting the proposal that memories are processed or consolidated in sleep. They claim too that their objections have largely been ignored, creating the impression that:

> the hypothesised role for sleep in memory is an established fact. (Vertes and Siegel, 2005)

Blakemore and Frith also note that many studies have shown the detrimental effect of lack of sleep on learning, citing examples where learning is less effective following poor sleep. They also refer to the positive effects that an appropriate amount of sleep can have on learning, describing a study by German researchers who found that sleep can inspire insights into problem solving:

> Volunteers in the study had to work out what the final number would be following a series of numbers. The order of the numbers, and hence the identity of the final number, was determined by two simple rules. However volunteers were not told about the rules. The sequence could be solved either by trial and error, or by working out the hidden rules. Volunteers were trained on the task and split into three groups. One group was retested after eight hours of being awake during the day. The second group was retested after staying awake overnight. The third group was retested after eight hours' sleep. After a night's sleep, almost twice as many volunteers gained sudden insight into the sequence rules than after eight hours of being awake. Sleep then, seems to facilitate insight into a newly acquired task. (Blakemore and Frith, 2005)

This is only one example from many studies that demonstrate the benefits for learning that sufficient sleep can bring.

Sleep and memory

Evidence about the impact of sleep on memory is less clear-cut. There is some agreement about the importance of memory in procedural skills, and a number of studies suggest that sleep consolidates the learning of motor skills. An imaging study that involved 12 young adults who were taught a sequence of skilled finger movements found a dramatic difference in the performance of those who were allowed to sleep during the 12-hour period before testing. Increased activity was found in the hippocampus and left cerebellum which support faster and more accurate motor output.

> Our findings indicate that storing a motor skill during sleep reorganises its brain representation towards enhanced efficacy. (Fischer and Changeux, 2005)

It has been suggested that this is one reason why infants need so much sleep, since learning motor skills is at its peak at this age.

There has been a substantial amount of research into different aspects of the impact of sleep on memory, and the picture that is emerging indicates that there is a relationship between them. A recent study provides a good example of the work that is taking place. In this case the researchers were investigating 'relational memory'. This is the flexible ability to generalise across existing stores of memory in the brain, and is seen as a fundamental property of human cognition. The study was designed to discover more about how and when this inferential knowledge emerges.

Fifty-six participants had varying amounts of sleep before the experimental task, which was to remember a set of 'premise pairs' (for example A>B, C>E). Unknown to them, the pairs contained an embedded hierarchy (A>B, B>C, C>D ...), and the real test was to see if the subjects picked up this implied knowledge – if they were in fact making 'inferential judgements'. After a short break, they were tested for retention of the pairs they had learned, and all achieved nearly identical results for this. However, when they were tested to see if they had detected the underlying hierarchy, the results were very different. Those who had had sufficient sleep showed 'highly significant relational memory', whereas those who were sleep-deprived showed little evidence of making such inferential judgements. (Smith and Squire, 2005)

Together these findings demonstrate that human relational memory can develop during breaks and time delays.

Lack of sleep alters the brain

Finally, an important study cited in *Nature/Neuroscience* suggests that sleep deprivation impairs memory for subsequent experiences by altering the function of the hippocampus, which is essential for memory. The researchers deprived one group of people of a night's sleep and then asked them to observe and remember a large set of picture slides for a subsequent recognition test. A control group did the same task, but after a good night's sleep. The researchers found that the sleep-deprived subjects showed decreased activity in the hippocampus, relative to the control subjects. The sleep-deprived group also had poorer subsequent recall abilities. The researchers suggest that sleep deprivation alters memory encoding strategies, and that sleep after learning is critical for the subsequent consolidation of human memory (Seung-Schik Yo et al., 2007).

 Point for reflection

How much sleep do your students feel they need and do they often get it? What hinders them from getting seven to eight hours sleep?

Pupils' views of memory

We turn now to pupils' views of memory taken from two surveys. We asked 300 pupils in one East London primary school several questions about remembering. Three quarters of the children thought they were good at it, and they reported using a range of successful strategies. On the other hand, the quarter who felt they were not good at remembering used quite different strategies from the successful ones, which we will return to in the final section.

Strategies used by the children

The pupils were asked which strategies for remembering they actually used. Just over a third said that they wrote things down and read them, which probably fits in well with the model of teaching and learning that they had experienced. Just under a third said that they would say things over and over again. This is unlikely to be very effective, because material learned in this way will probably stay in working memory for only a short time – but it is quite a reasonable strategy to use if you haven't had any discussion about memorising techniques. In response to a question about effective ways of remembering, about half the children felt that the best way was to 'have a go yourself', while the other half were divided between 'when someone shows you' or 'when someone tells you'.

There is one important caveat in relation to these answers: they were delivered outside any specific context, since the intention was that they would provide discussion material for teachers to work through with their classes. Despite this, they do illustrate the importance of talking with children about helpful ways of remembering so that they can develop more effective learning strategies.

In our second study, we asked about 1700 children in eight different primary schools what they did to help themselves remember things. About a tenth of them said that they didn't do any single thing in particular – somehow, they said, things just stayed in their heads. A few pupils felt that the content of what they had to remember was important. One child commented for instance, 'If it's a fun lesson, I remember things better'. Most children suggested a variety of strategies to help them remember. These included:

- writing things down (the most popular strategy);

- thinking about things again;

- saying things aloud or say it over in my head;

- making silly links to riddles, stories or chants;

- making up poems, raps, tunes or acronyms;

- asking someone/talking to someone about it;

- staring at it/reading it over/revising;

- listening carefully to the teacher;

- drawing a mental picture/visualising it;

- practising;

- drawing, for example spider web cartoons about it;

- reading and looking at classroom displays about it;

- shortening the words/splitting up the words;

- reading more/doing research about it;

- drinking water;

- giving a presentation on it;

- revisiting the actual place they learned about it.

These strategies are all useful to varying degrees, but as we shall see later there are better techniques for memorising than these pupils had yet come to appreciate. There is therefore a strong case for providing pupils with a choice of effective techniques for memorising that fit in with their own preferred learning strategies.

> ### Point for reflection
>
> What memory strategies do your pupils use? What evidence do they have that their strategies are successful?

What teachers could do to help pupils remember

In the larger of the two surveys, pupils were asked what they would do to help pupils remember if they were the teacher. The answers were thoughtful and imaginative. Almost half the children said that they would give more one-to-one help. They would use learning tapes, or take groups aside who didn't understand and give them tips on how to remember things. This is an important indicator that students would appreciate some guidance with memory strategies. Another suggestion was that they should be given the same sheet that the teacher was reading from so they could follow it – a very astute point!

Things that obstruct remembering

One further finding, connected to what gets in the way of remembering well, was that the pupils questioned felt that the teacher talking too much prevented them from doing their best work. I discovered my own weakness here when I gave the results to the teachers in the school, and set them a task in relation to the answers. No sooner had they started than I added a verbal qualification. Immediately one of the teachers remonstrated with me by saying that she couldn't think while I was talking, and that this is what we do to the children. The point was well made – it is important especially at the beginning of a task for pupils to have a clear thinking space and to allow their working memory time to assimilate any instructions.

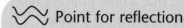

Point for reflection

Some pupils in the survey complained that noise in the classroom affected their concentration and ability to remember things. Ask some of your pupils to monitor noise levels and to note if you speak across their thinking time.

Differences between older and younger children

Returning to the main theme of memory, another question that was asked of the pupils in the first school was, 'How do you make the stuff that you learn stay in your head?' The responses were similar to those quoted above, but the spread of answers between the seven-year-olds (Year 3) and eleven-year-olds (Year 6) is interesting. In Year 3, pupils tended to give vague answers such as:

'I just remember.'

'It just sticks.'

'It just goes round and round in my head.'

In Year 6 the answers were more focused:

'I write it down.'

'I practise it again and revise it at home.'

Perhaps younger children need to be taught the basic strategies rather than just picking them up along the way. Strategies suggested and practised by the older children show that they really do think about remembering:

'I stare at it' – Year 5.

'I do a remember course' – Year 6.

'By listening carefully' – Year 6.

'I tell my parents and it helps me to remember' – Year 6.

'I take it in small steps' – Year 6.

Answers from individual children also sometimes suggested points for discussion. For example, in response to a question about the negative effects of playtime, one pupil said that after play he loses his memory, and 'I forget everything'! This may suggest that a brief point of reflection before the next activity could be helpful for some pupils.

Strategies for developing and improving memory

Clearly memory is an important intellectual skill – and some might say the most important – as it is the foundation for all other intellectual processes. We therefore need to consider carefully evidence-based techniques that that may help pupils to improve their memory strategies and their learning.

Music

Over the years, there has been a lot of discussion about the intellectual as well as aesthetic benefits of studying music. Anecdotal evidence has come from a range of sources, including the Suzuki method of teaching instruments and the Kodaly methods of teaching singing and sight reading. A recent study (Fujioka, 2006) from the University of Toronto suggests brain benefits for those pupils trained to listen to music on a daily basis:

> A clear music training effect was expressed in a peak of activity in the left hemisphere in response to violin sound in musically trained children compared with the untrained children.

It seems a neural network associated with sound categorisation and/or involuntary attention was established which could be altered by music-learning experience.

Memory improvement

A similar study, also from Canada, involved 12 children between the ages of four and six. Half of them attended a Suzuki music school throughout the year and were trained to read and understand music by this method; the other half were not given any music training outside school. After a year, the results showed that the musically-trained children had a greater improvement in general memory capacity as well as an improved ability to process sounds when compared to the other children. The study which was published in the journal *Brain* contained a note from the director. She said that while the improvement in the children's listening skills was not surprising, the improvement in memory was, and that it had not been predicted (Trainor, 2006).

Photographs

This study looked at the value of photographs as retrieval cues for young children. Fifty-seven children between the ages of three and eight participated in a fishing game. They were questioned about it ten days later, when some children were shown photographs and others were reminded verbally of what they had done. Those children who were shown the photos recalled more details than those who were just reminded (Aschermann, 1997). From this evidence it appears that visual cues can be an effective aid to retrieving stored material. Using visual cues such as pictures, diagrams and photographs in the classroom could help to improve children's memory for learning.

Reminiscing

Elaine Reese (2000) looked at reminiscing and recounting between pre-school children and their mothers. Reminiscing here refers to the recollection and retelling of past experiences, whereas recounting is narrating and enumerating the facts of an event one by one. Forty children between three and five participated in the experiment. It was found that mothers who provided more memory information during reminiscing, and who asked for more information during recounting, had children who reported more unique information about events. Reese concluded that parents can help their child remember by recalling events that they have shared and encouraging them to recall details about unshared events. These findings may not be surprising, especially when you consider the emotional power of the relationship between caregiver and child as outlined in the previous chapter. They reinforce the importance of this kind of shared reminiscence to the child's biography.

Working memory and unfamiliar words

A final study in this section, led by Susan Gathercole of the University of York, considers the importance of phonological working memory. The task of non-word repetition (CNRep) involves a child hearing a single novel word like 'pambor' and being required to immediately repeat it back. This occurs for 40 such items. Performance on this test is highly correlated with conventional tests of phonological working memory. The test is particularly appropriate for young children. They often hear unknown words and try to repeat them, so the task is familiar to them. A number of studies have consistently found poor CNRep scores in children who are poor readers and very low scores in children with reading difficulties. Adults with various language processing disorders also perform poorly on this test. Working memory capacity, which varies among individuals, affects many aspects of comprehension and recall. Among normal adults, working memory constraints usually only affect comprehension of particularly long and grammatically complex sentences. Among children, the ability to repeat back unfamiliar words affects both language comprehension and the learning of new words (Gathercole et al., 1994). The key finding here is that the ability of a child to repeat back unfamiliar words is constrained by the capacity of their working memory, and affects their ability to learn new words, as well as the ability to comprehend what they hear or read.

Evidence from many studies indicates that remembering is a skill-based activity that can be developed through learning and practising appropriate strategies. We will now consider some of the strategies that memory experts use to develop their skills and look for applications for pupils.

Memory strategies

One of the most successful memorisation practitioners in the UK is Dominic O'Brien. He has won the world memory championships eight times, was made a grand master of memory by the Brain Trust of Great Britain, and holds the world record for memorising a pack of 52 playing cards in less than three minutes. He has written many books on memorisation techniques and he has been known to memorise and recall – without any errors – approximately 50 shuffled packs of playing cards.

What attracted me to his strategies for improving memory was that they seemed to be in line with what we are now learning about the brain. For example, the main theme of this book is that learning is underpinned by attention and emotion. O'Brien's memory principles are similar. He emphasises the patterns of noticing through attention, and then uses novelty, imagination and emotion where possible, to commit ideas or objects to memory. He describes three steps for improving memory:

1 Making something memorable.

2 Storing an item in the mind.

3 Recall of the item at a future time. (O'Brien, 2005)

These steps involve both attention and emotion in order to encode the memory in the brain.

Key memory skills

There are three key skills that memory practitioners, including O'Brien, use, and these are based around association, location and imagination. These are the basic techniques and of course they can be combined together. Most children think that a good memory is a gift that some are blessed with and some are not. In fact, they need to know that their memories can be improved with good strategies such as these (just as we saw earlier in this chapter that they need to see their intelligence as plastic and therefore incremental). There are plenty of books describing techniques with these key skills (although I haven't referred to them directly here), and it is rather surprising that we have not made more use of them in schools.

Association

This technique makes use of natural and obvious links to make connections. Suppose you want to remember the name Mornington Crescent. Make a mental picture containing a sunrise (morning) with a heavy weight (ton) and a crescent moon (crescent). This technique fits well with memorising a group of objects on a shopping list. Association is a technique that is easy to use, and makes a good starting point with children for discussing memory strategies.

Location

This is another simple strategy that fits in to a narrative format. If you wake up in the night, for instance, and want to remember things to take to school like a calculator, trainers and homework, you can mentally put each object in a place that you will visit in the morning. You might imagine a calculator in the bathroom by the toothpaste, trainers in your bedroom by the light switch, and homework in the kitchen by the breadbin. These items are then connected to particular locations in your mind, and the memory for them is triggered when you visit those places in the morning.

Imagination

This comes naturally to children. If you want to remember to buy six eggs, create a dramatic picture. See yourself as a circus clown, with large feet and a clown's nose, and juggling six bright red eggs.

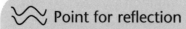 **Point for reflection**

If you are not familiar with these strategies, please try them with some things that you want to remember in order to test their usefulness.

Combining the three key skills

Here is one example to consider, where O'Brien suggests strategies for children who want to remember a past event in some detail. The exercise uses the three memory keys of association, location and imagination. The theme which is appealing to pupils is that of time travel.

1 The pupils choose a specific starting point which is familiar and personal, such as the school playground, or a special room where they spend time.

2 They try to connect people with this place – their voices, the way they laugh, certain mannerisms.

3 They try to hear the sounds they once heard in the place – a squeaky door, children playing nearby, traffic passing, any music around at the time.

4 They try to remember any smells that are associated with the place and what it was like to touch any of the surroundings.

5 They try to express what they felt at the time, and to think what it was that made them feel that way.

The aim of the time travel exercise is to take a child back to a location of the past, which will trigger a series of memories. Each visit generates more details of the event as one memory triggers another and fills out more details of the experience. This is a creative use of a child's mind to consolidate and bring into focus an aspect of their past. It builds on the familiar triangle of attention, emotion and memory, and combines them with imagination and sensory experience. It closely mirrors the early experience of infants and strengthens pupils' powers of recall, and should hold an important place in the curriculum. Developing strategies for memory with expert advice is a valuable and rewarding facet of intellectual development for pupils, and can underpin success within the subject disciplines. There is a parallel here to insights from Carol Dweck's work into pupils' understanding of their intelligence. The development of both memory and intelligence requires an understanding of neural plasticity.

Other areas where Dominic O' Brien's techniques could be useful and enjoyable for pupils, and which are described in his book, include:

- remembering names and faces;

- remembering directions;

- remembering spellings;

- remembering capitals and their countries;

- learning a foreign language;

- remembering the elements;

- the art of revision and maximising recall. (O'Brien, 2005)

Developing both memory and the brain

There is a burgeoning literature, and offers of web-based support, for all aspects of brain development. Much of this is directed at so-called 'grey panthers' – senior citizens whose numbers are increasing and who are a very receptive set of customers. One of the leaders in the market is the Japanese professor of neuroscience at Tohuku University, Dr Ryuta Kawashima. His book has sold over a million copies, and the small hand-held computer with games to stimulate and improve brain performance that accompanies it is massively popular around the world. His research shows that reading aloud, writing and solving simple calculations will activate the brain most effectively, and that these activities improve memory, creativity and communication skills. They also, he claims, slow down mental degeneration due to aging (Kawashima, 2005). Twenty years of observation and examining brain scans have led him to this simple conclusion: some activities use much larger areas of the brain than others. When we think, or problem-solve difficult calculations, or watch television, we use only a small part of the brain, but when we calculate quickly or read aloud we use much larger areas. His memory improvement techniques use these latter activities. The data supporting his view are rather limited and presented in such a way that his results cannot be checked, but there is other evidence as well.

His research team carried out work with elementary school students. They counted how many words the students could memorise in a minute, and found that on average they could manage 8.3 words. The same test was applied again after a two-minute calculation exercise, and the average increased to 9.8 words. This is a remarkable improvement in memory of around 20 per cent. (These data have yet to be checked and replicated.)

Another finding supporting Kawashima's ideas involved 12 Alzheimer's patients. The research team gave the patients a ten-minutes-a-day writing and oral reading exercise, and a ten-minutes-a-day calculation exercise to be carried out two to five times a week. The cognitive and pre-frontal cortex functions of non-participant control subjects deteriorated during the six months of the follow-up period. However, the participant subjects who did the exercises showed no such deterioration in their cognitive functioning – in fact, there was an improvement of their pre-frontal cortex function.

I have been using Kawashima's hand-held console for several months and I can detect improvements in my performance with some of the exercises. I also find the experience very enjoyable as the technology is well designed and it is a pleasure to use. One of the tests is a 'Stroop' test, where the names of colours are flashed on the screen and you have to give the name of the colour it is printed in, rather than what the word says. Practice with these tests certainly leads to improvement and increased speed. In my case, with a starting brain age of eighty, I could only get better!

By way of an end piece, I find the thoughts of Susan Engel on the complexity and the accuracy of memory have stayed with me:

> We now know that people build up neural pathways for memories and that the more often that particular memory is invoked, the more solid and strong that neural pathway becomes. We also know that the neural mechanisms that lead to memory are very similar to the neural mechanisms used for imagining things. This has suggested to some that there is a physiological basis for the complex interweaving of fact and fiction in people's personal recall. (Engel, 1999).

Pupils have a need to understand how memory has helped ̶
to evolve, and how it works in collaboration with attention an ̶
tion. They also need to know that, as with intelligence, men ̶
plastic and can be improved with training in the context o ̶
their brain works.

> Memory is reconstructed rather than retrieved. The job of the teacher
> then, is to foster this reconstruction – not simply pass out parcels of
> knowledge. (Brandt, 2000)

Some implications for learning from the themes in this chapter are:

- Memory can be influenced either positively or negatively by our emotions.

- Pupil's implicit and explicit memory are heavily influenced by the early environment that they have experienced.

- As Antonio Damasio notes, it is the composite of our memories that makes us uniquely who we are.

- Squire's three points for better memory work in school are helpful – purpose, enjoyment and using our whole personality.

- For young children, rhythm, rhyme, repetition and mnemonics and music will contribute to them developing their memory.

- Noticing is a key aspect of memory and links with findings about attention.

- Working memory can be improved with training.

- Individuals who perform at high levels in their discipline utilise specific kinds of memory process.

- Pupils need to be taught memory strategies as part of the curriculum.

If you are particularly interested in the theme of memory, the following books may interest you.

Memory: From Mind to Molecules – Squire and Kandel (2000)

This is a scholarly synthesis from two prize-winning professors who are accepted as grandmasters in the field of memory studies.

In this well-illustrated book, they examine memory from two sources. First, a biological study of how nerves signal to one another, where their key finding is that nerve cells act as elementary storage devices and thus they leave a record in the brain. Second, a study of brain systems and cognition, with their main finding showing that memory is not unitary but has different forms that use distinctive logic and different brain circuits. Although this is a technical book in some respects, it is very readable and informative.

How to Develop a Brilliant Memory – O' Brien (2005)

In contrast to the previous book, this is essentially practical, with 52 individual lessons each of which offers a practical strategy to improve your memory. Most of them are readily adaptable for use with pupils. There are exercises with tests so that you can see how your memory is improving. The author notes modestly that when he was at school he struggled with learning until he trained his memory. He has written an enjoyable and very useful book to share his techniques.

The New Brain – Restak (2003)

The author, a well known neurologist and neuropsychiatrist, expresses concerns about the impact of contemporary modes of living on the brain. He suggests that because the brain is plastic the modern age is rewiring our minds. He suggests that Attention Deficit Hyperactivity Disorder is the brain syndrome of our era. He explains that as the demands on the human brain increase, more and more children are experiencing symptoms of ADHD. The brain works best, he says, when it works on a single task for a sustained length of time rather than intermittent and alternating periods of time.

With regard to memory, he argues that a pill to perfect memory recall is not far away. However, he also suggests that this could prove a mixed blessing, for rather than recalling all the trivia of our lives, most of us really want to remember the important things related to our lives, like names, dates and issues to do with work or our social life. His is a highly readable and challenging account of the pressures of modern life and their possible impact upon the brain.

We now move to the final chapter where the wider implications of brain plasticity, learning and the curriculum are considered.

The social brain and brain plasticity

In this chapter we will explore the following:

- Our brains are social, as the brain is the organ most influenced on the cellular level by social factors. This has implications for the structure of learning experiences.

- Similarly, brain plasticity means that the brain is changed by thought and experience, which are important for learning.

- Mental rehearsal can create physical changes in the brain, and the effects of imagination and action are similar in the brain.

- Paying attention is essential to brain plasticity.

- Brain decline occurs when we cease to learn.

- Brain performance is enhanced with exercise (see Ratey (2008)).

- Studies show that meditation has benefits for the brain, including the ability to focus.

- Pupils need to understand how their brains work to help them with effective strategies, and to inform their decisions about substances as they grow up.

- Pupils should engage in discussing the quality of life and learning in school in order to improve things.

- Studies of happiness and wellbeing may have positive benefits for pupils and teachers.

Introduction

I have a burning memory from the time when I was a teacher in Camden Town in London. One day, nine-year-old Mario said to me, 'Do you like children, Sir?' I often reflected on what his question said about the quality of my relationships with pupils. The truth is that within the clamour of a crowded curriculum it is easy to overlook the importance of engaging with pupils' thoughts and feelings about what is happening around them. This can result in an unsatisfactory learning environment for them, and a social experience which prevents them from reaching their full potential. There may also be ramifications outside the classroom which can impact on society more widely – but as the eminent educator Basil Bernstein once said, 'education cannot compensate for society'.

Recent research has raised perturbing questions about levels of happiness among British children, and has also suggested that pupils' well-being should be higher up the educational agenda. Perhaps the most worrying results came in UNICEF's 2007 report 'An Overview of Child Well-being in Rich Countries: Commentary from York and Stirling Universities'. The researchers looked at indicators in education, health, relationships, housing and safety from 25 European states. Pupils from the UK finished in the bottom eight in three-quarters of the categories. Overall they came twenty-first, above only Slovakia and the three Baltic states, despite Britain being one of the wealthiest countries in the EU.

Three findings stand out:

- 44 per cent of UK pupils had been in a fight in the past year – the seventh highest rate among the 25 states;

- only 43 per cent of under-18s in the UK found their peers kind and helpful;

- UK pupils came twenty-first out of the 25 states when measured on their attitude to education, including how much they liked school. (Stewart, 2006)

Tellingly, for school achievement UK pupils were ranked ninth. But when taking into account factors that measure educational wellbeing (such as the number of young people not in education, employment or training), the UK dropped to twentieth place overall. The figures also showed the UK ranked at the top for a number of social problems,

including children living in families where one or mor
not in work.

It would be facile to imagine that a greater focus on
could combat basic social inequity. Nevertheless there is comp
evidence about the impact of exercise and meditation on wellbeing, as
well as the importance of social interaction and lifelong learning. This
chapter then, is devoted to aspects of brain study that have implications for pupils' wellbeing and learning in school.

Brain plasticity and the implications for learning

The discovery that the brain is plastic and not hard-wired has created
the possibility of profound new understandings about learning. In
the past twenty years scientists have shown that the brain is highly
adaptive in adults and remains so throughout life, and that consequently there are implications for lifelong learning. Plasticity comes
into play at the deepest levels of brain structure. In response to the
right stimuli, neural connections can be rewired, the brain's grey
matter can thicken and new neurons can be produced. As we shall
see, these effects can have life-changing possibilities.

The origins of these breakthroughs are described in a recent book *The
Brain That Changes Itself*, by the psychiatrist and researcher Norman
Doidge. He argues that the notion of the neuro-plasticity of the brain
is a revolutionary concept which gives hope to those with serious lim-
itations, and opens up new vistas for our understanding of learning.
He does this through the description of a number of exceptional case
histories of individuals whose lives have been transformed (Doidge,
2007). He refers to one case where a woman felt as if she was falling
over all the time, and because she felt this way, she did indeed fall
over. Her vestibular system was retrained and she was able to walk
normally again. This was possible because it is the brain that inter-
prets what the eyes see, and the brain is plastic and can be changed.

Imagination – we are what we think!
Doidge also gives accounts of several investigations that have implications for our understanding of learning. Alvare Pascual Leone, a
neuroscientist at the Harvard Medical School, specialises in the use of
trans-cranial magnetic stimulation (TMS). With this mechanism he
can stimulate areas of the brain and cause behavioural change; for

example, stimulus to a brain area that can cause a finger to move. He studied how people learn new skills by using TMS to map the brains of blind subjects learning to read Braille. He found that the Braille-reading fingers had larger maps in the brain than other digits, and also noted that the motor maps in the brain increased in size as the subjects increased the number of words per minute that they could read. Both of these effects were predictable.

There was, however, one surprising discovery that has implications for the learning of any skill, and this was in the way that the plastic changes occurred over the course of each week. He found that these were different on a Friday and a Monday. From the start of the study, the Friday maps showed expansion, but by Monday they had returned to baseline size. The Monday maps showed an opposite pattern. They didn't begin to change until six months into training, then they increased slowly and reached a plateau at ten months. At the end of ten months the students took two weeks off, and when they returned their brains were re-mapped. These maps were unchanged from the final Monday mapping two months before. Daily training had led to dramatic short-term changes during the week, but over the weekends and months more permanent changes were seen on Mondays.

> Pascual Leone believed that the differing results on Monday and Friday suggest differing plastic mechanisms. The fast Friday changes strengthen existing neuronal connections and unmask buried pathways. The slower and more permanent Monday changes suggest the formation of brand new structures, probably the sprouting of new neuronal connections and synapses. (Doidge, 2007)

In effect, this work suggests that after a brief period of practice, perhaps as when we cram for a test, it is relatively easy to improve performance because we are strengthening the existing synaptic connections. However, we may forget what we have crammed because these neuronal connections, quickly made, are just as quickly unmade. Making a skill permanent requires the slow, steady and patient work that forms *new* connections. So the tortoises who seem slow to pick up a new skill may nevertheless learn it better than the hares, who won't necessarily hold onto what they have learned without the sustained practice that solidifies their learning.

Mental rehearsal creates physical change
Pascual Leone's next experiments with mental practice involved two groups of students who had never studied playing the piano. He

taught them a sequence of notes, showing them which fingers to move and letting them hear the notes as they were played. The first group sat in front of an electric piano keyboard two hours a day for five days, and imagined both playing the sequence and hearing it played. A second 'physical practice' group actually played the music over the same time scale. Both groups had their brains mapped before the experiment, each day during it, and afterwards. Then each group was asked to play the sequence, and a computer measured the accuracy of their performance. Pascual Leone found that both groups learned to play the sequence, and that both showed similar brain map changes. He was surprised to find that the mental practice alone produced the same physical changes in the motor system as actually playing the piece on a piano. By the end of the fifth day the changes in motor signals to the muscles were the same in both groups, and by the third day the 'imagining' players were as accurate as the actual players were. Clearly then, as Doidge points out:

> mental practice is an effective way to prepare for learning a physical skill with minimal physical practice.

 Point for reflection

In what ways, could you use mental rehearsal with your students to enhance their learning?

Think hard and be stronger

A final experiment in this section showed that imagining using muscles can actually strengthen them. This study, cited by neuroscientist Ian Robertson, looked at the effects of mental versus real practice in tensing and relaxing one finger of the left hand. There were three groups – a control group who did nothing, a group who did exercises and another group who just imagined doing the exercises. This took place for five sessions a week over four weeks, a total of 20 training sessions in all. At the end of four weeks, the finger strength of each person was compared with people in the control group who did not train at all. The physical practice group's finger strength had increased by 30 per cent, while the control group showed no change in strength. However, the group who imagined the exercise increased their strength by 22 per cent which is very close to the amount of the increase of those who actually did the work physically (Robertson, 1999).

The notion of plasticity then, embraces the fact that the neuronal circuits that are created by imagining are almost identical to those created by actual practice. This is not new: athletes, gymnasts and performers in many different arenas have been making use of mental rehearsal for some time, particularly in playing chess as we shall see further on. It may be a process that we could make more use of in schools.

Paying attention is essential to plasticity

We turn now to the work of Michael Merzenich, who has been described by Ian Robertson as the 'world's leading researcher on brain plasticity'. In the course of his work with both humans and monkeys, Merzenich discovered that paying attention is essential to long-term plastic change. In numerous experiments, he found that lasting changes occurred only when the monkeys paid close attention:

> When the animals performed tasks automatically, without paying attention, they changed their brain maps, but the changes did not last. We often praise the ability to multi-task, but while you can learn when you divide your attention, it doesn't lead to abiding change in your brain maps. (Doidge, 2007)

This echoes a major theme from Chapter 3, showing yet again how important *focused* attention is for brain development. Merzenich has also examined autism, improving reading skills and the development of the aging brain. In this last field he has radical views, and believes the learning of new skills should be a part of everyone's aging process. In particular, he commends the learning of new languages.

A young head on old shoulders?
There are many products available that claim to help keep the brain active and stave off dementia for our fast-increasing aging population. Merzenich and the scientists at Posit Science design brain fitness programs, and they have a different stance from most others in their understanding of plasticity. Merzenich thinks that our neglect of intensive learning as we age leads the systems in the brain that modulate, regulate and control plasticity to waste away. He laments the fact that drugs worth massive amounts of money are being used to produce only four to six months of improvement in brain performance for the elderly. This, he says, neglects what the brain needs to develop new skills and sustain abilities. Common problems among the elderly, for example of difficulty with finding words, often occur because of the

gradual neglect and consequent atrophy of the brain's attentional system and nucleus basalis (an area which undergoes degeneration during Alzheimer's Disease). These have to be engaged for plastic changes to occur. Merzenich explains that, as we age, our brains get noisier and cluttered because they are not being properly exercised, and this is why we have trouble remembering, finding and using words:

> We have an intense period of learning in childhood. Every day is a day of new stuff. Then in our early employment, we are intensely engaged in learning and acquiring new skills and abilities. So more and more as we progress in life we are operating as users of mastered skills and abilities. (Doidge, 2007)

By the time we reach our seventies, we may not have systematically engaged the systems in the brain that regulate plasticity for perhaps some fifty years. This is a very important insight that recasts the purposes for learning in school. Learning for life takes on a different meaning when we consider the deterioration that can take place if the life-enhancing and essential nature of learning is neglected.

Often learning is framed in instrumental terms such as 'learn this in order to pass an exam', but this research helps us to see a purpose for continuous learning – which is essential to the maintenance of the quality of our lives and a necessity rather than an optional extra. The rewards for following what is a very stringent programme of learning new skills are considerable. With 50 hours of training, a study reported in the *Proceedings of the National Academy of Sciences*, a shift of performance in memory tests from the level of a seventy-year-old to that of people in the forty to sixty age range was noted (Merzenich et al., 2006).

As we are learning to extend the longevity of our bodies, we also need to consider how to nurture and sustain our brains, and an understanding of brain plasticity is central to this concern. For their futures, children need to be taught this wider perspective of learning to extend and enhance their active lives. If even half of what Merzenich is finding about plasticity is true, we need to reframe our notions of retirement in terms of continuous education and challenge.

Learning to create new brain circuits – Constraint Induced Movement Therapy (CI)

Another aspect of brain plasticity has been exploited for powerful benefits by the behavioural neuroscientist Dr Edward Taub, who created the healing known as Constraint Induced Movement Therapy (CI). This is really a family of therapies that teaches the brain to rewire itself after physical damage to the body. So, for example, if the left arm is affected by a stroke and is unable to move, the right arm is strapped so that it can't move, and the patient has to focus on the left arm to rebuild the brain map. Studies have demonstrated that after a stroke the brain map for an affected arm shrinks by about a half, so a stroke patient has only half the original number of neurons to work with.

Two studies confirm that CI therapy restores the reduced brain map. One measured the brain maps of six stroke patients who had had arm and hand paralysis for an average of six years. After CI therapy, the size of the brain map that governed hand movement doubled. The second study showed that the changes could be seen in both hemispheres of the brain, demonstrating how extensive the neuroplastic changes were (Doidge, 2007).

Can genius be created?

This provocative question based around the plasticity of the human brain derives from the extraordinary story of the gifts and upbringing of Susan Polgar, now a grandmaster at chess. Susan and her two younger sisters, Grandmaster Judit and International Master Zsofia, were part of an educational experiment carried out by their father Laszlo Polgar, who sought to prove that children could make exceptional achievements if trained in a specialist subject from a very early age. His thesis was that geniuses are made rather than born. He and his wife educated their three daughters at home, with chess as the main specialist area. They were also taught Esperanto. Laszlo had studied the life of Mozart, and was convinced that genius was the result of hard work plus fortunate circumstances. The girls' brains were engineered for chess, with six hours of work each day to learn 100,000 chess chunks (patterns of pieces on the board). With constant repetition, the patterns were moved from the working memory into the long-term memory. At the age of fifteen, in 1984, Susan became the top-ranked female player in the world and was the first woman to earn the title of International Grandmaster.

One feature of brain plasticity is that neural networks can be developed to, as it were, colonise areas normally used for other purposes. This is true of Braille readers for example, and the self-taught German mathematical expert Rudiger Gamm, who was found to have developed five more brain areas for calculating than 'normal' people (Doidge, 2007). Susan Polgar was found to have made use of the fusiform gyrus (part of the temporal lobe concerned with face recognition), and was thus able to store the mass of information about dispositions of pieces on the chess board. Whether this qualifies as genius or not is a source of continued debate on the internet blogs, but it is significant that both of her sisters and her two children have also achieved highly in the upper reaches of international chess. This implies that high-level skills can be taught.

A brain plasticity summary

- Imagination and action have similar effects in the brain.

- Mental rehearsal can be valuable for some activities.

- Brain circuits can be expanded to overcome damage.

- Thoughts can change the material structure of the brain.

- Paying close attention is necessary for long-term plasticity changes.

- Keeping the brain healthy throughout life requires constant major learning, not just in school and further education.

 Point for reflection

Are there any curriculum areas where your students could experiment with mental rehearsal and the use of using their imagination to support their learning?

We now turn to the question of exercise, a major consideration for brain health.

The brain thrives and develops with physical exercise

The notion of *mens sana in corpore sano* has long been embedded in the school curriculum at some level, but it has special relevance for pupils in the twenty-first century. It was only a hundred years ago that physical education (PE) in elementary school was connected with military drill. As Alan Penn explains, 'the controversy between military drill and the more benign physical exercises had not been resolved by the time war broke out in 1914' (Penn, 1999). Perhaps there is still some perception of PE being prescriptive because of its resonance with our past history. It is even more of an issue now, when we have an evidence base about the brain showing how vital it is, and yet the subject has low status in an overcrowded curriculum.

Today there is a new imperative for children to have regular exercise of some kind, which is as much to do with the health of their brains as with their bodies. The bigger picture of what prevents children from having enough exercise, right from birth and on through childhood, is clearly presented by Sue Palmer in *Toxic Childhood* (2006). She explains how 'fear turns children into couch potatoes'. She notes that from the very earliest stages of life, children won't get adequate exercise unless they have time lying on their fronts and sitting up in baby seats, and goes on to list the many constraints that children experience as they grow older. Foremost is the impact of the technologies available in the home, and the anxiety parents feel about allowing their children to play outside. Other factors include diet, a fear of the sun, fewer opportunities to walk because of the dominance of cars and a lack of places to play. Sue reports research from Scotland where three-year-olds weigh much more that their counterparts of 25 years ago because of their lack of exercise. Similarly, a recent newspaper report cites research showing that 'children of the seventies did twice as much exercise' as the children of today (Fleming, 2006).

The physical effects of lack of exercise are now becoming clear, with increases in cancers, diabetes and heart disease being among the most dramatic. The impact on the brain is equally important, but less well understood.

Depression and self-esteem

John Ratey is a prolific writer about the brain and he particularly focuses on the benefits of exercise. He describes the first gain as being the increase in blood going to the brain, which augments the number and density of blood vessels in the areas that need them most. He relates this to two other gains – an increase in self-esteem, and a lower chance of developing depression. The latter gain was demonstrated in a study of depression involving 1,000 subjects. Men who burned 2,000 calories a day in exercise were 30 per cent less likely to develop clinical depression than less active men (Ratey, 2001). In his current work devoted to exercise and the brain, he underlines the importance of sport.

> The idea of the scholar athlete isn't just about marketing, it goes back to the culture of ancient Greece where fitness was almost as important as learning itself. Aerobic exercise helps the heart pump more blood to the brain, along with the rest of the body. More blood means more oxygen and thus better nourished brain cells. People have been slow to grasp that exercise can affect cognition. (Ratey, 2008)

The benefits of brain exercise

Many studies show a wide range of brain benefits for older people through exercise, but only a few have investigated the effects on the young. Current concerns about the 'baby boomer' generation who are now approaching retirement have led to the development and marketing of many commercial programmes. These include one promoted by Baroness Susan Greenfield, arguably our best known neuroscientist. Her programme includes improvements to reaction times, short-term memory, memory recall and eye-to-hand co-ordination.

Voluntary exercise

Important evidence about the effects of exercise on brain activity in children comes from Charles Hillman, assistant professor at the University of Illinois. He provides a very important review of the field in a paper entitled 'The Neurobiology of Exercise'. This utilised a team of 18 researchers from the USA and Australia (Hillman, 2006), with the main findings illustrating that:

> voluntary physical activity and exercise can favourably influence brain plasticity

and also that:

> motor skill training and regular exercise enhance executive functions of cognition and some types of learning.

Here we have a clear connection with learning. This is amplified in a *Newsweek* article based on Hillman's work and that of others in this field, where some of his research is explained. Hillman took 259 pupils in the third and fifth grades (aged nine to eleven years old). He measured their body mass index and put them through basic exercise routines. He then checked their physical abilities against their math and reading scores on standardised tests (Carmichael, 2007). He concluded that, when taking socio-economic status into account, there was a clear relationship between fitness and attainment.

Hillman and other researchers in the field of exercise used brain-scanning tools and a sophisticated understanding of biochemistry to explore what lay behind this apparent relationship. They realised that the mental effects of exercise were more profound and complex than they had previously thought. The process starts in the muscles. Every time a bicep or quad contracts and relaxes, it sends out chemicals that travel through the bloodstream and into the brain. One of these, a protein called IGF-1, increases the production of chemicals in the brain, including one in particular that is central to our thought processes – brain-derived neurotrophic factor (BDNF). Ratey calls this molecule 'Miracle-Gro for the brain'. It fuels almost all the activities that lead to higher thought (Ratey, 2008).

The feature of this work that is most important for teachers and parents to understand is that with regular exercise the body builds up its level of BDNF. The brain's nerve cells start to branch out, join together and communicate with each other in new ways. This is the process that underlies learning. Every change in the junctions between brain cells may signify a new fact or skill that has been acquired and stored, and BDNF makes that process possible. The neuroscientist Fernando Gomez explains that a brain that is low on BDNF shuts itself off to new information. Lab rats in his experiments spent weeks running on a wheel which caused their BDNF levels to increase. He then left half of the group alone, while he blocked the BDNF effect by using a drug with the other half. He next subjected both groups to a test where they had to discover an underwater object. The first group had no difficulty, but the BDNF-deprived group were distinctly slower and less successful (Gomez-Pinilla et al., 1995).

A final point from the *Newsweek* article is that in the USA many educators are pushing for an overhaul of physical education in public schools. In Kentucky, there is legislation for all pupils to have 30 minutes of exercise each day, up to the eighth grade, while in Illinois (where Hillman's research took place) students with poor verbal skills have started taking PE immediately before their reading class. John

Ratey says that already they have found improvements in performance (Carmichael, 2007).

Neurogenesis

Until comparatively recently it was thought that the brain was more or less a fixed entity with a basic complement of neurons, and that therefore intelligence was fixed. However, recent studies have shown that the brain can create new neurons. This is the process of neurogenesis. The work of Fred Gage at the Salk Institute showed that after working out for three months all the subjects in his experiments appeared to grow new neurons. Co-author Scott Small, a neurologist from the Columbia University medical centre, explained:

> Those who gained the most in cardiovascular fitness also grew the most nerve cells. This too might be BDNF at work, transforming stem cells into full grown functional neurons for the first time. In terms of trying to understand what it means, the field is just exploding. It was extremely exciting to see this exercise effect for the first time. (cited in Carmichael, 2007)

This research is still at an early stage, but there are as many implications for children's brains as there are for adults. Phil Tomporowski, Professor of Exercise Science at the University of Georgia, explains:

> Exercise probably has a more long-lasting effect on brains that are still developing. A good workout or session of football can have a widespread effect on children's brains. (cited in Carmichael, 2007)

There is the important issue here also that pupils who get into good exercise habits at home and school may well continue them later in life, and stave off the illnesses that inactive adults are prone to.

The Gage neurogenesis experiments were with animals, and due caution must be exercised when extrapolating from the findings and applying them to children, but it is worth bearing in mind that the effects were seen only when the exercise was voluntary. Voluntary exercise is characterised not only by absence of stress, but also by the presence in the brain of theta waves. These are also found during acts of attention. In a recent book which we will be considering carefully in the next section, the researcher Fred Gage told the Dalai Lama that the voluntary component could be the key to the promotion of neurogenesis (Begley, 2007).

In the UK, physical education is often seen as a low-status, Cinderella subject because teachers are more concerned about other areas of the curriculum that will be assessed in inspections. The emerging evidence about the connections between exercise and brain health make it paramount that we review the place of exercise in the school curriculum and accord it higher status.

From what we have looked at so far, we can sum up the following:

- Physical exercise is fundamental for a healthy brain.

- Parents need to consider exercise opportunities for their children as an essential part of each day.

- Teachers need to provide exercise opportunities over and above playtime on a daily basis.

- It may well be that for some lower achieving children, exercise is vital for attainment as well as for wellbeing.

 Point for reflection

There are many benefits to pupils' brains from undertaking physical exercise. What other opportunities, in addition to the prescribed curriculum, might benefit your students?

We move now to consider the benefits for the brain of what is almost the opposite of physical exercise – meditation.

Meditation and neuro-feedback for learning

When I was a head teacher I was often in school for evening events, and I found that around 5 pm my energy seemed to run out. I took a course in transcendental meditation, not for any spiritual purpose but just to see if it would help with improving my energy levels. It worked well – after just 20 minutes of meditation I felt completely refreshed. There are other benefits from meditation, and a number of US universities have been conducting studies to discover what advantages it can bring to the brain. It may be that meditation, perhaps as part of extra-curricular activities, could benefit pupils with regard to both their learning and their general wellbeing.

In a study conducted at Massachusetts General Hospital, 20 Buddhist meditators were compared with a control group of 15 people who had had no experience of yoga or meditation. MRI scans were taken, and the researchers studied detailed images of the participants' brains. They found that regions of the meditators' brains involved with the attentional focus were thicker than those of the non-meditators. They also found that in an area associated with the integration of emotional and cognitive processes, differences in cortical thickness were more pronounced in older participants, suggesting that meditation could reduce the thinning of the cortex that typically occurs with aging. The area where these differences were noted is involved in the modulation of functions like heart rate and breathing, and also in the integration of emotion and cognition. This work was carried out in 2005 and the researchers stressed then that the results need to be validated by longer-term studies (McGreevey, 2005).

Recent studies on meditation are now adding this more precise information, as in a two-stage experiment concerning the emotions from University College, Los Angeles. The researchers used fMRI to scan the participants' brains to see which parts were active or inactive at any given time. Thirty subjects were asked to look at pictures of male and female faces making emotional expressions. Below each photo was a caption containing words describing an emotion, such as 'angry' or 'fearful', or two possible names for the people in the picture, one male and one female. The subjects were asked to pick the most appropriate emotion or gender name to fit the face they were looking at. When they chose labels for the negative emotions, activity in the right ventrolateral pre-frontal cortex region – an area associated with thinking in words about emotional experience – became more active, whereas activity in the amygdala, a brain region involved with emotional processing, was calmed. By contrast, when the subjects picked appropriate names for the faces, the brain scans revealed none of these changes. This suggests that only emotional labelling makes a difference in the brain.

In the second stage, 27 of the same subjects completed questionnaires to determine how 'mindful' they were. Meditation and other 'mindfulness' techniques are designed to help people pay more attention to their present emotions, thoughts and sensations without reacting strongly to them. Meditators often acknowledge and name their negative emotions in order to let them go. When the team compared brain scans from subjects who were more mindful with those who were less so, they found a stark difference. The more mindful subjects experienced greater activation in the right ventrolateral pre-frontal cortex, and a greater calming effect in the amygdala after labelling their emotions. The psychologist who led this second part of the study believes that the findings may help to explain why mindfulness meditation programmes improve mood and health (Wenner, 2007).

Meditate to concentrate

Another recent study from the University of Pennsylvania suggests that meditation may help to improve attention. The study (led by a neuroscientist) examined how meditation might modify three subcomponents of attention:

- the ability to prioritise and manage tasks and goals;

- the ability to focus on specific information;

- the ability to stay alert to the environment.

Participants performed tasks at a computer that measured response speeds and accuracy. At the outset, retreat participants who were experienced in meditation demonstrated better executive functioning skills, as well as the cognitive ability to focus, manage tasks and prioritise goals. On completion of the eight-week training, participants new to meditation had greater improvement in their ability to move and focus attention quickly and accurately (orienting). After the one month's intensive retreat, the new participants also improved their ability to keep their attention better focused. The results suggested that meditation, even for as little as 30 minutes a day, may improve attention and focus for those with heavy demands on their time. The attention performance improvements that come with practice may, paradoxically, allow us to become more relaxed (Jha, 2007).

These studies are by no means conclusive, but they do suggest that meditation can cause changes to the brain, thereby improving some aspects of performance.

 Point for reflection

Meditation can take many forms, from a few moments for reflection to a sustained peaceful focus for longer periods. Are there any aspects of your pupils' learning where some form of meditation or quiet time for reflection might be valuable? Which might these be?

Neuroscience, meditation and Buddhist monks

One study of a different kind involved a collaboration between the Dalai Lama and some of his monks who had had substantial experience of meditation. There was also a group of meditation experts and neuroscientists from the University of Wisconsin, led by Richard Davidson and sponsored by the Mind and Life Institute (see www. mindandlife.org). Davidson's hypothesis, built around his previous work in the field, was that

> meditation or mental training can exploit the brain's plasticity and produce changes ... that underlie happiness and other positive emotions. (Begley, 2007)

All of the Buddhist adepts had practised meditation for at least 10,000 hours and had also been on retreat for three years, during which time they had lived apart from society and had passed most of their waking hours in meditation. Davidson built up a unique database of recordings of the brain waves and brain activation patterns of these monks. The broader findings with regard to happiness are discussed in the next section, but the focus here is on outcomes from the data of Matthieu Ricard, a French-born monk. He was not only actively involved in the design of the study, he also experienced both fMRI and EEG scanning from a geodesic net with 256 sensors. He was asked to engage in pure compassion, which focuses on 'unlimited compassion and loving kindness to all human beings'.

One surprising effect stood out in these recordings – the registering of gamma waves. In fact the increase in gamma activity was larger than had ever been reported in neuroscience. Brainwaves of this frequency are believed by scientists to reflect the activation and recruitment of neuronal resources and mental effort. They also indicate neuronal activity that integrates a wide range of brain circuits. Davidson found that the more hours of meditation training a monk had had, the stronger and more enduring the gamma signal was. The control group, who had had a full week of such training, showed a slight increase in gamma signal.

One of the main conclusions from this significant piece of research is that mental training that engages concentration and thought can alter connections between thinking and the emotions. Inevitably, there is a great deal to learn in the future about this kind of work in terms of social and learning issues, and of its relevance for pupils in the twenty-first century.

We will now move on to consider the study of brainwaves and its potential to support learning.

Neuro-feedback and brainwaves

Neuro-feedback is a means of training brainwave activities through monitoring the electrical activity of the brain for particular purposes (other names for this process are neurotherapy and biofeedback). It is an area to be regarded with caution because the evidence base is as yet quite limited, but there are accounts of positive work with subjects who have been diagnosed with various conditions. In the USA, for example, it has proved possible for pupils with ADHD to avoid taking the drug Ritalin.

Perhaps the best known use of brainwaves is where patients manipulate letters and words on a computer screen or where a child can make an aircraft rise up on a computer screen. This latter example was given in the *Scientific American Mind* magazine to illustrate how neuro-feedback 'may ease symptoms of ADHD, epilepsy and depression and even to boost cognition in healthy brains (Kraft, 2006).

There is little evidence as yet about the connections between brainwave states and learning, but there are indications that some people learn more effectively in the alpha state. Certainly for children who are highly distractible, training in using the alpha state could be valuable. An interesting study by Ruth Olmstead showed that the use of auditory and visual stimulation improves the performance of pupils with learning difficulties (Olmstead, 2003). An article in the *Independent* also reported that she had created a sound machine to overcome her own Attention Deficit Disorder. The machine, called 'MindSpa', was designed to train the brain to use different brainwave patterns. She used this with 30 children with attention problems who had had very low scores on intelligence tests. Over a six-week period they had twelve 35-minute sessions designed to calm their erratic brain activity:

> 'These were children who didn't like school, weren't successful and had very low self-esteem,' says Olmstead, 'but when I retested them after the treatment, every single child showed a significant improvement.' (Usborne, 2007)

Wise voices would warn us to beware of single studies which haven't been replicated, but this is an area of study that could produce great benefits for children, and it deserves further development.

Another major theme that follows from meditation and brainwaves is the value for pupils of understanding more about their brains.

Pupils' understanding about their brains and the impact of substance abuse

There are two important reasons why pupils should be taught about their brains.

- To help them to appreciate how their brains work so they can have a better understanding of their own strategies for learning.

- To enable them to appreciate the impact of substances on their brains and to inform their choices and decisions as they grow up.

With regard to the first of these, I am all too aware of how over-crowded the curriculum is at present, but understanding how the brain functions could still contribute to pupils achieving more. The following suggestions for some areas to cover are just an outline.

- How the brain develops from birth.

- Neural migration and neural pruning, ie., the formation and shaping of the brain.

- A journey round the brain and its main parts.

- Brain cells and how they communicate.

- The senses.

- Attention and its value.

- Thoughts and feelings.

- Why the brain is greedy for oxygen and the importance of exercise.

- How memory works.

- Working definitions of intelligence and preferred learning strategies.

www.neuroscienceforkids.com is an excellent website for pupils. It is managed with regular updates by Dr Eric Chudler, and has high quality diagrams and pictures that can be used in schools. In a chapter on 'Drug Use and Abuse', Jeanne Pierre Changeux (a professor at the Pasteur Institute) explains that drug use to affect conscious states in humans goes back almost to the origins of humanity (Edelman and Changeux, 2001). He notes that the pollen of eight medicinal plants was discovered, intentionally deposited, in a 60,000-year-old tomb in Iraq. While clarifying in detail the impact that drugs can have on the brain, he argues that a compulsive use of drugs is:

> a universal human fact and a tragic reality of today's society that most governments have failed to control. (Edelman and Changeux, 2001)

He also believes that preventive policies must address the social and economic causes, and that education has to have an influential role to play here.

The neuroscience writer and biologist Robert Sylwester suggests that a shift in education is needed:

> Since our knowledge of the biochemistry and effects of drugs has now dramatically increased, school drug education programs should go beyond the moral overtones and effects of drug use to a stronger focus on clear explanations of what drugs are, how they and their addictive properties work and how to live intelligently with them. (Sylwester, 2004)

Susan Greenfield is uniquely placed to comment on the issue of drugs, as she is a pharmacologist as well as a neuroscientist. In her challenging work *Tomorrow's People*, she made a prophetic comment:

> As I write this, the UK is teetering on the edge of decriminalizing cannabis, perhaps even legitimizing it completely. Instead of coming to terms with, if not circumventing the difficulties of life, we increasingly seek the chemical equivalent of shutting our eyes and putting our hands over our ears. (Greenfield, 2004)

Several brain issues converge at this point and lead on to the next theme. Children understanding their brains and knowing about strategies to improve their wellbeing or happiness are both connected with the competence to deal with the range of stimulants and depressants that are available to them.

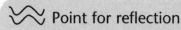

Point for reflection

How do you feel about teaching your pupils a basic knowledge of their brains, so that they can make best use of them both for studying and for making choices when they are older in regard to substances? Is there a forum with their parents to discuss the implications of this work?

Wellbeing – happiness and learning in school

The argument for happiness to be considered in schools is strongly put by Paul Martin:

> The case for happiness to feature prominently on the educational agenda is compelling. Making happy people is rarely an explicit aim of education, let alone its prime purpose. Schools are geared up to deliver measurable academic achievement, not something fluffy and intangible like happiness … The implicit belief seems to be that education and happiness have little to do with one another. (Martin, 2005)

He focuses on the importance of a lifelong love of learning and argues that that we should therefore cultivate children's intrinsic motivation at school. He reasons that a love of learning remains central to happiness and health. This is certainly true in terms of keeping our brains active and healthy.

The psychologist Csikszentmihalyi was one of the first writers to describe what was needed to achieve happiness with his concept of 'flow'. It is not possible to condense his brilliant work here as it is so complex. However, he did himself explain that 'flow' is concerned with having skills and being able to express them in a particular way, and he makes clear that this involves being and interacting with others since we are 'social animals'. He cites the Latin phrase for being alive as *inter hominem esse* ('to be among men'), whereas *inter hominem esse desinere* ('to cease to be among men') was to be dead (Csikszentmihalyi, 2002).

Martin Seligman, another psychologist, has done more than anyone else to establish positive psychology and the study of happiness as valid areas of study. He focuses on our signature strengths, by which he means the unique individual strengths that we each have as the basis for a fulfilling life. As with Csikszentmihalyi, he does not believe that the pursuit of pleasure should be the route forward:

> Habitually choosing pleasures over the gratifications may have unto-ward consequences. (Seligman, 2002)

One of the main elements in Martin Seligman's work is his investigation of the continuum between optimism and pessimism. He believes that both are learned behaviours because we take them from our caregivers (Seligman, 2006). He tackles this at root through what he terms the ABC system – A stands for adversity, B for the belief that underpins it, and C for the consequences. The ABC procedure is useful in examining actual situations from school life. He shows how it is possible to work through such incidents, and over time to learn to make more optimistic choices. This, and other strategies for dealing with feelings, should be connected with and lead to improvements in learning.

The social brain

Another important dimension related to wellbeing is the social construction of the brain:

> The social brain is defined by its function – namely the brain is a body organ that mediates social interaction while also serving as the repository for those interactions between brain physiology and the individual's environment. The brain is the organ most influenced on the cellular level by social factors. (Bakker et al., 2002)

We saw this in Chapter 4 when we looked at the emotions. The highly regarded neuroscientist and psychotherapist Allan Schore explained that:

> The beginnings of living systems set the stage for every aspect of an organism's internal and external functioning throughout the lifespan. (Schore, 2003)

In other words, we build our intellectual development from the framework of our early interpersonal experience.

Using the social brain for school improvement

Pupils' sense of wellbeing in school could be strengthened if we engage with their thoughts and feelings of what is happening around them, and if they understand how their learning and social experience might be improved. In the surveys that we carried out asking for pupils' views of life and learning in school, there were two things that stood out. The first was the quality of the pupils' perceptions and the constructive way in which they were given, and the second was how some teachers either couldn't see the point of the exercise or couldn't make the shift needed to engage with pupils on this issue. Yet, despite the fact that they felt under real pressure because of their accountability, all the heads and teachers who took part registered an appreciation of what they learned from pupils. This included those few who weren't convinced of the point of the exercise.

In the single school study of 300 pupils, it was clear that social relationships regarding their learning were influential in the pupils' lives in both positive and negative ways. For example, when they were asked what made them happy in class nearly half chose the answer, 'My friends', and when asked what made them unhappy in class, almost a third chose, 'Some people'.

Pupils and teachers talking about wellbeing and learning

When asked what stopped them from working better, more than a third chose the response, 'Talking to my friends'. This prompted some of the teachers to start discussions with their pupils about how they could reasonably engage in social chat that didn't interfere with learning-based talk. The onus here was on the pupils to figure out ways in which this might happen, rather than leaving teachers to work out all of the disciplines and routines.

In another eight-school study there were two sets of questions on the questionnaire. The first was a basic set devised by the teachers in the project for all the pupils, and the second was for each individual school. In the first set there was a generic question about learning: 'What stops you from learning or working better?' More than two thirds of pupils from the eight schools chose the response, 'People talking to me or distracting me while I am working'. In total 1718 pupils answered this question, so it would seem that talking to friends in lessons is a crucial area for class discussion. Using pupils' responses as a basis for discussion can lead them to consider their own responsibilities for the quality of the working/learning environment.

Another of the generic questions was 'What makes you feel unhappy in class?' Almost a third responded that 'Unkind or annoying classmates' were the cause of unhappiness. They observed that their activities included name-calling, passing nasty notes, and telling lies about them. In addition, they mentioned hurtful behaviour when no one would play with them, when people pushed or hurt them, and when people swore or gave them rude finger signs. All this forms part of the routine – hidden or under-the-cover action – which teachers do not necessarily see but many pupils experience, and it can prove both distressing and a distraction from learning. An opportunity to discuss these issues and consider how to deal with these as a class community can have a real impact on pupils' learning and wellbeing.

Bette McCallum, the project researcher for this study, noted that more than a fifth of the pupils said that they got stressed about work and dreaded some subjects. They worried when they couldn't understand what to do, and felt pressurised when given spot questions, when working in tests or against the clock. Some also explained that they simply felt inadequate. She gave two examples:

> 'I feel unhappy when you try your utmost best and a teacher says it is not good enough.'
> 'I feel unhappy when people say, "I've done all the questions. How many have you done?" That makes me feel sad because I don't usually finish.' (McCallum, 2004)

Five hundred and sixty-two pupils were unhappy when there was conflict in the classroom, when they were at odds with neighbours or friends, or when it was too noisy and the teacher was shouting. Children also disliked being told off in front of others and became unhappy when they could see that other children were upset.

Three points emerged from these comments:

- A large number of pupils in the study see learning in school as about being right or wrong. This may be a reflection of a culture where, as Watkins and Lodge note:

> the emphasis on test results and performance rather than on learning, reinforces a view that only experiences to enhance test performance are important. (Watkins and Lodge, 2007)

It denies the importance of seeing learning as a process of making meaning, where errors and mistakes are a valuable part of working towards accuracy and understanding

- Children are very sensitive about other people's comments, and this can get in the way of their learning. This should be on the agenda for class discussion as a means of bringing the experience into the open, and to find ways through this in order to focus more on learning.

- Teachers know how to communicate their subject matter in a one-way direction, but a real two-way exchange of views and ideas with pupils does not come so easily to all. This may seem unfair when teachers have so much pressure just to manage the subjects on the National Curriculum, and yet the kind of 'responsive and attentive listening' described by Seligman, is something most of us crave (Seligman, 2002). It could certainly reduce some of the anxieties described above. There is some superb guidance on this issue (that I wish I had known about as a teacher and parent) in *How To Talk So Kids Will Listen and Listen So Kids Will Talk* (Faber, 2001).

 Point for reflection

Are there discussion opportunities with your pupils where the issue of the behaviour of others constraining learning can be addressed?

Happiness or wellbeing?

Seligman uses these terms interchangeably, while acknowledging that happiness is concerned with life as a whole, and wellbeing with home and school. Apprehension over pupils' wellbeing is not just the concern of educators, as a letter to the *Daily Telegraph* citing the views of a range of writers, scientists and educators, makes clear:

> Since children's brains are still developing, they cannot adjust as full-grown adults to the effects of ever more rapid technological and cultural change … they need first hand experience of the world they live in and regular interaction with the real-life adults in their lives. (Editor, 2006)

One of the contributors to this letter was Susan Greenfield, cited in the last section. In her view:

> we are creating a society where people have problems differentiating between reality and the cyber world. Children who spend most of their time in front of a screen are bombarded with information at a very fast pace.

She reminds us that:

> information is not knowledge, intelligence comes from relating one fact to another, in seeing connection where nobody has seen one before. (cited in Bowditch, 2006)

Technology and wellbeing

Technology is one factor that has an effect on wellbeing, as we explored in Chapter 3 with regard to the impact of television on children's brains. The omnipresent factor though – 'the elephant in the classroom' – is our feelings in relation to learning, and how we feel about what is happening in the learning environment. The work of Martin Seligman indicates some possible ways of taking pupils' feelings into account. He and his colleagues established the Penn Resiliency Project (PRP) fifteen years ago. It is a school-based curriculum, designed to build resilience, promote adaptive coping skills and teach effective problem solving. There have been controlled studies in the USA, China and Australia involving 2,000 eight-to fifteen-year-olds, and it has been found effective in helping to buffer children against the effects of stress, anxiety and depression (see info@pennproject.org). It is also backed by many organisations, including the Young Foundation, whose Director Geoff Mulgan says:

> Over the last few years, there has been a huge amount of emphasis on exams and a huge amount of money going into school buildings, but almost no emphasis on children's well-being. We're not claiming that this is a magic solution, but PRP is one of the most verified projects of its kind. (cited in Morrison, 2007)

The foundation is supporting a project where resiliency lessons are being used in 21 secondary schools from three local authorities for a three-year period. One of the key supporters of so-called 'happiness lessons' is the headmaster of Wellington College, Dr Anthony Seldon. I made a visit to the school to talk about brain studies and learning, and I was very impressed by the quality of mutual respect between teacher and pupils. PRP is also supported by the Labour peer Lord Layard, who expresses particular concern for those in society suffering from anxiety and depression. He estimates that this costs society £75 billion per year, and argues that a climate of individualism, consumerism and a preoccupation with celebrity and money are preventing children from achieving happiness. We were warned about this possibility by the academic David Hargreaves, who in the 1980s wrote about the 'culture of individualism':

> The fault with the culture of individualism, let me repeat, does not lie with the humanistic sentiments and ideals which it enshrines. The error lies in the repudiation of the nineteenth century concerns with the social functions of education and the attempt to substitute individual functions in their place ... The consequence is that we fall into what I shall call the fallacy of individualism. This is the belief that if only schools can successfully educate every individual pupil in self-confidence, independence and autonomy, then society can with confidence be left to take care of itself. (Hargreaves, 1982)

An understanding of the nature of our social brain and the elements of wellbeing may well suggest that an awareness of service to others is an essential ingredient of a 'good' education.

If you would like to know more about the themes in this chapter, the following books may be helpful:

The Brain that Changes Itself – Doidge (2007)

The whole field of brain plasticity is explored in this work, through a series of moving case studies. They include accounts from two women, one of whom was born with half a brain which rewired itself to work as a whole. In the second narrative, a woman who was labelled as retarded describes the processes she underwent to heal her learning disorders, and how she then became a teacher. She founded a school in Toronto and offered brain exercises to help others. Doidge provides a hopeful portrait of the endless adaptability of the human brain and some valuable insights into its functioning.

Train your Mind, Change Your Brain – Begley (2007)

This work also takes up the theme of our extraordinary ability to transform ourselves through brain plasticity. Begley emphasises the importance of attention, reminding us that:

> without attention, information that our senses take in – what we see and hear, feel, smell and taste – literally does not register in the mind. It may not be stored even briefly in the memory. What you see is determined by what you pay attention to.

The Dalai Lama, in his introduction, affirms that:

> The research presented here confirms that deliberate mental training can bring about observable changes in the human brain.

The repercussions of this, he asserts, will be of practical importance to our understanding of education and mental health. In showing how mental activity changes the brain, the author, a well-respected science writer, cites many positive examples of the benefits of meditation. It is therefore a valuable source for educators.

Authentic Happiness – Seligman (2002)

Seligman's first book in the field of positive psychology was *Learned Optimism* in 1990. Since then he has refined his ideas into practical programmes which are evident in this book. He discusses brain studies which relate positive moods to activity in the left frontal lobes of the brain. He also notes survey evidence which shows that that the average mood while watching television is one of mild depression. The main thrust of the book both for children and adults is the understanding of what he terms our signature strengths, such as integrity, honesty and open-mindedness, and he argues that satisfaction derives from using signature strengths in our everyday lives. He provides practical ways for children to begin to identify their strengths and to use them more in their lives.

Here are some questions to consider, based on the evidence in this chapter.

- What are the implications of the 2007 UNICEF report for pupils in your care and how might it be connected with attainment?

- Brain plasticity suggests that we all have the potential to improve our performance to some extent. Strategies in this book suggest starting points; for example, the fact that the use of imagination and action are close together in the brain. Mental rehearsal is one such strategy – how might you use it with your pupils?

- Do your students see learning as just for school or can they see it as an essential tool for life that can help to stave off Alzheimer's and dementia?

- Exercise is essential for brain wellbeing and performance at all stages of life. Daily exercise is not an option, but an essential. Do all of your pupils appreciate this?

- Studies show that meditation has many benefits, including managing tasks, focusing and staying alert. How might your pupils take advantage of this?

- Learning about the brain is beneficial for pupils in two important ways – it can help them to use their brains more effectively for study and it can help them to make informed choices about the use of substances. Can you use either or both of these approaches?

- Would Seligman's studies of optimism and pessimism be useful for your students?

- Can surveys be valuable as a means of finding out what pupils feel about life and learning in school and for making school improvements?

- Which areas of life and learning in your school would you like to find out about from your pupils?

In conclusion, some of the main themes from this book are emphasised in the next section with themes for professional development.

Appendix: suggestions for some themes of professional development

The ideas below are noted as starting points for teachers who wish to explore further the themes of attention, emotions and memory, either for themselves or with their pupils, as part of their continuous professional development.

1 Attention and learning

The full range of practices that contribute to attention include noticing, observing, orienting and screening out unwanted information. Evidence shows that *focused* attention helps pupils to gain more from their learning experiences, and that simple exercises can lead to improvements. These can be used with all ages, but some adjustment may be needed to ensure they are appropriate for younger children.

The activities suggested below could help pupils to develop an awareness of some of the important issues surrounding attention, as well improving their attention skills.

Focusing on and describing simple objects

Ask pupils to look carefully at their hand or an object such as a leaf or a stone, and note as many different features as they can. Get them to record their observations in a variety of forms, such as writing notes, drawing a pen or pencil portrait or sketch, taking a photograph, or making notes to be recorded on computer or CD.

Noticing and observing

Take pupils for a walk in the local environment and ask them to focus their attention on a particular building or a specific feature of the local environment. Consider simple ways to record what they notice and observe, and perhaps feed back this to another group. As with all of these suggestions, this could be part of a more extended piece of work.

Maintaining attention to tasks

Jane Healy suggests a five-point plan to help pupils manage their tasks, through asking themselves these questions.

1 Check that you understand the task and identify the problem in words.

2 What is my plan? Talk through the possible steps to a solution.

3 How should I begin? Analyse the first step.

4 How am I doing? Am I on task?

5 Reflect back on the task, analyse the results. How did I do?

Developing an awareness of the limitations of multi-tasking

Arrange for pupils to attempt to carry out two activities simultaneously; for example, drawing and talking, or tapping with one hand while writing their name. The aim is to notice what happens and how difficult it is for the brain to divide attention. It is not that we can't do two things at once, but there is a cost. Homework in particular needs to be done one item at a time. Discussion of the issues that arise will be as important as the exercise itself.

Understanding the dangers of too much exposure to television

Encourage pupils to keep logs or to find other ways to be aware of their watching time as a basis for discussing the balance in their lives of passive and active activity. It seems that most of us imagine that we watch television rather less than we do, so it needs some effort to note the actual amount of time that we devote to our viewing habits. This may also lead to a discussion of the use of technology in the bedroom and the need to set boundaries in order to ensure sufficient sleep in preparation for learning. There is no suggestion here (or in this book generally) that watching television is inherently bad: instead the issues are around the choice of programmes and the quantity of time that we spend in front of the television.

Some points for teachers to consider

Performance and learning goals

Performance goals are convergent and concerned with finding the 'right' answer that the teacher has designed the activity to achieve. However, learning goals are concerned with helping pupils to learn about their learning strategies and thus to become more effective learners. Both are important, but there should be a balance of concern for each one. Consider the balance of both learning and performance goals in your planning.

Modelling and imitation

Consider the opportunities in each curriculum area that your pupils have for imitating and modelling that will help them with their learning. Think about ways in which any improvements could be measured, and not least in terms of pupils' attitudes to their work.

Recognising the risks of over-using computers

The strategies suggested by Healy in Chapter 3 (see page 53) may be helpful as a guidance framework for both teachers and parents.

2 The emotions and learning

There are four guiding principles that inform our understanding of the emotions and their importance for learning:

1   Motivation is the force that connects the emotions and action.

2   The emotions are fundamental to all communication.

3   Touch is important for physical and emotional growth.

4   Movement is profoundly connected with emotion.

Some points for teachers to consider

Role play and drama are important for connecting the emotions with learning. Activities that engage pupils with both the content of study and role play/drama should be provided across the curriculum.

Movement related to curriculum themes should be used where possible to help with enhancing and consolidating learning.

Reference to the emotions should be included as part of the work in most of the curriculum. This should include both the student's emotions and those of the people being studied. This in turn involves a shift in planning teaching to seeing the brain and body as an integrated system and then planning to take this into account.

Pupils' understanding of the purpose for an activity is important because if teachers give their pupils a lucid explanation of why they are being asked to carry out an activity, there is more chance that the pupils will be motivated. Some teachers deal with this through the use of success criteria. An understanding of purpose affects the quality of the outcome from the pupil.

Anxiety and stress can have an impact on performance. Opportunities to discuss feelings in relation to tasks can be very productive, and this is more important than is currently appreciated. Once we see that emotions cannot be separated from the intellect, then it becomes clearer that feelings are important to the quality of the outcome.

Pupils' views of their intelligence

The work of Carol Dweck shows how important and influential pupils' own views of their intelligence can be. Discussion around the themes of what makes you think you are intelligent or clever or not bright – or whatever pupils think about their performance – can be very important, but needs sensitive handling in small groups. Many pupils have a deficit view and helping them to consider the evidence they have for this is worthwhile.

The ability to get on with others in school has been identified as a positive trait for learning. Teachers might consider how pupils can discuss the characteristics and qualities of those who are easy to get on with, or what constitutes a hindrance.

3 Memory and learning

It is important for each pupil to understand that memory, like intelligence, is plastic and that it can therefore be improved with training.

Pupils' views of their strengths and weaknesses with memory are worth exploring in order for them to assess their influence, since memory is an important influence on learning.

Relating activities to pupils' own background and experience, particularly in the early stages of education, is valuable for reinforcing memory.

Working memory is essential to pupils for many reasons, but particularly when holding information from instructions about a task. A small number of pupils have difficulty with this and will need to be identified in order for suitable help to be given. Some pupils mask this problem by seeking help from their friends or the pupils they sit with. This is a coping strategy that can in itself be stressful.

The effects of sleep on memory would be a useful area of discussion for pupils, particularly for those who have computers and televisions in their bedrooms.

Strategies for remembering, including those that pupils already use themselves, can be a very useful topic for discussion, leading to an appreciation of more and less successful approaches. Teachers may wish to experiment with and test strategies based on the three key memory skills of association, location and imagination. The work of Dominic O'Brien, described in Chapter 5, provides one of many models for helping pupils with techniques for the following:

1   Remembering names and faces.

2   Remembering directions.

3   Remembering spellings.

4   Remembering countries and their capitals.

5   Learning a foreign language.

6   The skills of revision and recall.

A multi-sensory approach to developing memory can be valuable. Teachers may choose to experiment with ways to involve one or more of the senses to assist in recall.

4 Physical fitness: the new PE

One of the major themes in this book, explored particularly in Chapter 6, is that exercise is essential for brain growth. Many brain studies show that this is true at any age. A recently published work by John Ratey provides a lot of new evidence and further arguments in support of exercise. The essential shift that is taking place is away from games skills and towards personal fitness. This is particularly needed in our culture where technology can lead towards sedentary occupation. Ratey explains how exercise improves learning at three levels:

1 It optimises the mind-set to improve alertness, attention and motivation.

2 It prepares and encourages nerve cells to bind to one another which is the cellular basis for logging new information.

3 It stimulates the development of new nerve cells from stem cells in the hippocampus. (Ratey, 2008)

In light of this evidence, teachers could consider how the curriculum can encourage shifts towards an emphasis on personal fitness for pupils that does not deny the possibilities for enthusiasts of playing games.

Conclusion

These ideas are offered as starting points, because they underpin some of the shifts in our understanding of learning as indicated by neuroscience. I hope you find something useful among them as an action point for your particular situation and your pupils.

References

Amini, F., Lewis, T. and Lannon, R. (2000) *A General Theory of Love*. New York: Random House.

Aschermann, E. (1997) 'Memory strategies in young children', *Applied Cognitive Psychology*, 12: 55–66.

Athey, C. (1990) *Extending Thought in Young Children*. London Paul Chapman.

Bakker, C., Gardner, Jr., R., Koliatsos, V., Kerbeshian, J., Looney, J. G., Sutton, B., Swann, A., Verhulst, J., Wagner, K. D., Wamboldt, F. S. and Wilson, D. R. (2002) 'The social brain: a unifying foundation for psychiatry', *Academic Psychiatry*, 26: 219.

Baron-Cohen, S. (2004) *The Essential Difference*. Harmondsworth: Penguin.

Baginsky, M. (2000) Policy Practice and Research Series. London: NSPCC.

Bateson, G. (1972) *Steps to an Ecology of Mind*. New York: Ballantine.

BBC (2007) 'The ghost in your genes', *BBC Science and Nature*.

BBC News (2006) Friday 24 February, Child anxiety link to ecstasy.

BBC News/Health (2007) Lasting genetic legacy of the environment. Medical notes – Monise Durrani. BBC website.

Begley, S. (2007) *Train Your Mind, Change Your Brain*. New York: Ballantine.

Blackwell, L. (2007) 'Implicit theories of intelligence', *Child Development*, 78 (1): 246–62.

Blakemore, C. (2001) 'Early learning and the brain'. RSA lectures.

Blakemore, S. and Frith, U. (2005) '*The Learning Brain*'. Oxford: Wiley-Blackwell.

Blakeslee, S. (1997) 'Studies show talking with infants shapes the ability to think', *New York Times*, 17:14.

Bowditch, G. (2006) 'Inside the mind of a brain expert', *Sunday Times,* 26 February.

Bransford, J. and Cocking, R. (2000) *How people learn*, National Academy Press.

Brandt, R. (1998) *Powerful Learning*. Alexandria, VA. A.S.C.D.

Brierley, J. (1987) *Give me a child until he is seven*. Abingdon: Routledge Falmer.

Bruer, J. (1996) *The Myth of the First Three Years: A New Understanding of Early Brain Development and Lifelong Learning*. New York: Free.

Bruer, J. (1997) 'Education and the brain: a bridge too far', *Educational Researcher,* 26 (8): 4–16.

Butterworth, B. (1999) *The Mathematical Brain*. Basingstoke: Macmillan.

Carmichael, M. (2007) 'Can exercise make you smarter?' *Newsweek,* March 26.

Carter, R. (1998) *Mapping the Mind*. London: Weidenfeld & Nicolson.

Chi, M. (1983) 'Network representation of a child's dinosaur knowledge', *Developmental Psychology*, 19: 29–39.

Chugani, H.T., Behen, M. E., Muzik, O., Nagy, F., Juhasz, C. and Chugani, D. C. (2001) Local brain functional activity following early social deprivation: A study of post-institutionalized Romanian orphans'. *NeuroImage* 14: 1290–1301.

Cotman, C. and Berchtold, N. (2002) 'Exercise: a behavioral intervention to enhance brain health and plasticity', *Trends in Neurosciences*, 25 (6): 295–301.

Covington, M. (1999) 'Caring about learning', *Educational Psychologist* 3(2): 127–36.

Crossman, A. and Neary, D. (2005) *Neuroanatomy*. Amsterdam: Elsevier.

Csikszentmihalyi, M. (2002) *Flow: the Psychology of Optimal Experience.* Surrey: Rider.

Damasio, A. (1994) *Descartes' Error.* Emotion, Reason and the Human Brain: New York: Vintage.

Damasio, A. (1999) *The Feeling of What Happens.* London: Heinemann.

Damasio, A. (2003) *Looking for Spinoza–Joy, Sorrow and the Feeling Brain.* London: Heinemann.

Demos, J. (2005) *Getting Started with Neurofeedback.* New York: Norton.

Department of Education and Science (DES) (1967) Children and their Primary School (Plowden Report). London: HMSO.

Dewey, J. (1938) *Experience and Education.* New York: Collier.

Diamond, M. (1998) *Magic Trees of the Mind.* Harmondsworth: Penguin.

Dickinson, E. (1968) *A Choice of Emily Dickinson's verse.* London: Faber and Faber.

Dishman, R., Berthoud, H. R., Booth, F., Cotman, C., Reggie Edgerton, V., Fleshner, M., Gandevia, S., Gomez-Pinilla, F., Greenwood, B., Hillman, C., Kramer, A., Levin, B., Moran, T., Russo-Neustadt, R., Salamone, J., Van Hoomissen, J., Wade, C., York, D. and Zigmond, M. (2006) 'Neurobiology of exercise', *Perspectives–The North American Association for the Study of Obesity,* 14:345–56.

Doidge, N. (2007) *The Brain that Changes Itself.* New York: Viking.

Draganski, B., Gaser, C., Busch, V., Schuierer, G., Bogdahn, U. and May, A. (2004) 'Neuroplasticity: changes in grey matter induced by training', *Nature Neuroscience,* 427: 311–12.

Dugatkin, L. (2000) *The Imitation Factor: Evolution Beyond the Gene.* New York: Free.

Dweck, C. (2000) *Self-Theories.* London: Psychology Press.

Edelman, G. (1992) *Bright Air, Brilliant Fire.* Harmondsworth: Penguin.

Edelman, G. and Tononi, G. (2000) *Consciousness – How matter becomes imagination.* London: Allen Lane.

Edelman, G. and Changeux, J. P. (2001) *The Brain.* Piscataway, NJ: Transaction.

Edelman, G. (2006) *Second Nature Brain Science and Human Knowledge.* Yale: Yale University Press.

Editor (2006) 'Modern life leads to more depression among children, *The Daily Telegraph,* 12 September.

Egan, K. (1988) *Primary Understanding–Education in Early Childhood.* London: Routledge.

Eisner, E. (2002) *The Arts and the Creation of Mind.* Yale: Yale University Press.

Ekman, P. (2003) *Emotions revealed.* New York: Times Books.

Eliot, L. (2001) *Early Intelligence – How the Brain and Mind develop in the First Five Years of Life.* Harmondsworth: Penguin.

Elliot, J., Templeton, S. (2007) *Sunday Times.* Times online news. 18 March.

Ellenbogen, J. (2007) 'Human relational memory requires time and sleep', *Proceedings of the National Academy of Sciences, USA.*

Elliott, J. (2006) 'Multitasking children are losing the plot', *The Sunday Times,* 26 March.

Engel, S. (1999) *Context is Everything – The Nature of Memory.* London: Freeman.

Entwhistle, H. (1970) *Child Centred Education.* London: Methuen.

Ericsson, K. (2002) *Attaining Excellence Through Deliberate Practice: Insights from the Study of Expert Performance.* Hillsdale, NJ: Erlbaum.

Ericsson, K., Krampe, R. T. and Tesch-Römer, C. (1993) 'The role of deliberate practice in the acquisition of expert performance', *Psychological Review,* 100: 363–46.

Eriksson, P., Perfilieva, E., Bjork-Eriksson, T., Alborn, A., Nordborg, C. and Peterson, D. (1998) 'Neurogenesis in the adult hippocampus', *Nature Medicine,* 4 (11): 1313–17.

Faber, A. and Mazlish, E. (2001) *How To Talk So Kids Will Listen and Listen So Kids Will Talk.* London: Piccadilly.

Feinstein, D., Eden, D. and Craig, G. (2005) *The Healing Power of EFT and Energy Psychology.* New York: Piatkus.

Fischer, S., Nitschke, M. F., Melchert, U. H., Erdmann, C. and Born, J. (2005) 'Motor memory consolidation in sleep shapes more effective neuronal representations', *Neuroscience,* 25 (49): 11248–55.

Fleming, N. (2006) 'Children of the seventies did twice the exercise', *The Daily Telegraph,* 25 February.

Foreman, M. (1990) Mother Goose. London: Walker.

Franke-Gricksch, M. and Leube, K. (2003) You're One of Us – Systemic insights and solutions for Teachers, Students and Parents. Heidelberg: Carl-Auer – Systeme Verlag.

Freeman, W, J. (1999) *How Brains Make Up Their Minds.* London: Weidenfeld & Nicolson.

Fujioka, T., Ross, B., Kakigi, R., Pantev, C. and Trainor, L. J. (2006) 'One year of musical training affects development of auditory cortical-evoked fields in young children', *Brain,* 129 (10): 2593–608.

Gathercole, S. Willis, C., Baddeley, A. and Emslie, H. (1994) 'The chilren's test of non word repetition', *Memory,* 2: 103–27.

Gerhardt, S. (2004) *Why Love Matters*: How Affection Shapes a Baby's Brain. Brunner: Routledge.

Goldberg, E. (2001) *The Executive Brain – Frontal Lobes and the Civilized Mind.* Oxford: Oxford University Press.

Goldberg, E. (2005) *The Wisdom Paradox.* New York: Free.

Golman, D. (1995) *Emotional Intelligence.* London: Bloomsbury.

Gomez-Pinilla, F., Neeper, S., Choi, J. and Cotman, C. (1995) 'Exercise-induced increase in brain-derived neurotrophic factor in the rat brain', *Nature,* 373 (109).

Gopnik, A. and Kuhl, P. (1999) *How Babies Think.* London: Weidenfeld & Nicolson.

Grady, C., Springer, M., McIntosh, A. and Winocur, G. (2005) 'The relation between brain activity during memory tasks and years of education in young and older adults', *Neuropsychology,* 19 (2): 181–92.

Greenfield, S. (1996) *The Human Mind Explained.* London: Cassell.

Greenfield, S. (1997) *The Human Brain.* London: Weidenfeld Nicolson.

Greenfield, S. (2000) *The Private Life of the Brain.* London: Allen Lane.

Greenfield, S. (2000) *Brain Story.* London: BBC.

Greenfield, S. (2004) *Tomorrow's People.* Harmondsworth: Penguin.

Greenspan, S. (1997) *The Growth of the Mind.* New York: Perseus.

Greenspan, S. and Shanker, S. (2004) *The First Idea – How symbols, language and intelligence evolved from our primate ancestors to modern humans.* Cambridge MA: Da Capo.

Gregory, R. (1998) *The Oxford Companion to the Mind.* Oxford: Oxford University Press.

Gregson, L. (2007) *Early Years' Matters 13 – Learning and Teaching in Scotland.* Online Newsletter.

Griffin, I.C. and Nobre, A.C. (2005) 'Saporin impairs excitatory and inhibitory eye blink conditioning'. *The Journal of Neuroscience.* pp. 2731–2.

Grubin, D. (2002) *The Secret Life of the Brain: Episode Three: The teenage brain*. PBS home video.

Hall, D. (2003) *Resilience – Giving Children the Skills to Bounce Back*. Available at: www.voices for children

Hannaford, C. (1995) *Smart Moves*. Great Ocean.

Hargreaves, D. (1982) *The Challenge for the Comprehensive School*. London: Routledge & Kegan Paul.

Harlow, H. F. (1958) 'The nature of love', *American Psychologist*, 13: 573–685.

Healy, J. (1990) *Endangered Minds*. New York: Touchstone.

Healy, J. (1998) *Failure to Connect*. New York: Simon and Schuster.

Healy, J. M. (2004) 'Early television exposure and subsequent attention problems in children', *Pediatrics* 113 (4): 917–18.

Hebb, D. (1949) *The Organization of Behaviour*. New York: Wiley.

Howard, P. (1994) *The Owner's Manual for the Brain*. Austin TX: Leornian.

Howe, M., Courage, M. L. and Edison, S. (2003) 'When autobiographical memory begins', *Developmental Review: Lakeshead University*, 23: 471–94.

Iacoboni, M., Gallese, V., Mazziotta J., Molnar-Szakacs, I., Buccino, G. and Rizzolatti, G. (2005) 'Grasping the intentions of others with one's own mirror neuron system', *Public Library of Science*, 3 (3).

James, S. (2004) *Baby Brains*. London: Walker.

Jensen, O., Gelfand, J., Kounios, J. and Lisman, J. (2002) 'Oscillations in the alpha band increase with memory load in a short term memory task', *Cerebral Cortex*, 12 (8): 877–82.

Johnson, M. (2005) *Developmental Cognitive Neuroscience*. Oxford: Blackwell.

Kandel, E. (2006) *In Search of Memory*. New York: Norton.

Kappelou, O. Counsell, S., Kennea, N., Dyet, L., Saeed, N., Stark, J., Maalouf, E., Duggan, P., Ajayi-Obe, M., Hajnal, J., Allsop, J., Boardman, J., Rutherford, M., Cowan, F. and David Edwards, A. (2006) 'Abnormal cortical development after premature birth shown by altered allometricscaling of brain growth', *PLOS Medicine*, August.

Kawashima, R. (2005) *Train your Brain – 60 Days to a Better Brain*. Harmondsworth: Penguin.

Klein, B., German, T., Cosmides, L. and Gabrial, R. (2004) 'A theory of autobigraphical memory', *Social Cognition*, 22 (5): 460–90.

Klingberg, T., Olesen, P. and Westerberg, H. (2004) 'Increased prefrontal and parietal activity after training of working memory', *Nature Neuroscience*, 7 (1).

Kraft, U. (2006) 'Train your brain', *Scientific American Mind*, 17 (1).

Le Doux, J. (1998) *The Emotional Brain*. New York: Touchstone.

Le Doux, J. (2002) *Synaptic Self*. Harmondsworth: Penguin.

Lipton, B. (2005) *The Biology of Belief*. New York: Mountain of love/Elite.

Lynch, V. (2001) *Emotional Healing in Minutes*. London: Thorsons.

MacLean, P. (1990) *The Triune Brain in Evolution*. New York: Plenum Press.

Maguire, E., Frackowiak, S. J. and Frith, C. D. (1997) 'Recalling routes around London: activation of the right hippocampus in taxi drivers', *Neuroscience*, 17 (18): 7103–10.

Martin, P. (1997) *The Sickening Mind – Brain, Behaviour, Immunity and Disease*. London: Flamingo.

Martin, P. (2005) *Making Happy People*. New York: Fourth Estate.

Maslow, A. (1971) *The Farther Reaches of Human Nature*. Harmondsworth: Penguin.

Matthews, P. and McQuain, J. (2003) *The Bard on the Brain*. Washington DC: Dana.

McCallum, B. (2004) *Switch on to learning 2*, St James' Junior School, Tunbridge Wells, TN2 3PR.

McEwan, I. (2006) *Saturday*. Vintage.

McGreevey, S. (2005) 'Meditation associated with structural changes in the brain'. Available at: www.eurekaalert.org/pub

McLeod, P. and Rolls, E. (1998) *Introduction to Connectionist Modelling of Cognitive Processes*. Oxford: Oxford University Press.

Meadows, S. (1993) *The Child as Thinker – The Development and Acquisition of Cognition in Childhood*. London: Routledge.

Merzenich, M., Mahncke, H., Connor, B., Appelman, J., Ahsanuddin, O., Hardy, J., Wood, R., Joyce, N., Boniske,T. and Atkins, S. (2006) 'Memory enhancement in healthy older adults using a brain plasticity-based training program'. *Proceedings of the National Academy of Sciences, USA*, 103 (33): 12523–28.

Mind Gym (2005) *The Mind Gym*. New York: Time Warner.

Mithen, S. (1996) *The Prehistory of the Mind*. New York: Phoenix.

Morrison, J. (2007) 'The pioneering technique that's helping to combat depression in the classroom', *The Independent*, 19 July.

Mortimore, P. (2006) *An Education System for the 21st Century*. London: National Union of Teachers.

Mujtaba, T. (2001) 'Switch on to learning', Colegrave Primary School, London, E15 1JY.

O' Brien, D. (2000) *Learn to Remember*. London: Ducan Baird.

O'Brien, D. (2005) *How to Develop a Brilliant Memory*. London: Duncan Baird.

OECD (2002) *Understanding the Brain: Towards a New Learning Science*. Paris: Organisation for Economic Cooperation and Development.

Ofsted (2007) *The Foundation Stage: A Survey of 144 settings* (HMI No 2610). London: HMSO.

Olmstead, R. (2005) 'Use of auditory and visual stimulation to improve cognitive abilities in learning disabled children', *Journal of Neurotherapy*, 9(2) 49–61.

Orlinsky, D. E., and Howard, K. I. (1986) *Process and Outcome in Psychotherapy*. Wiley: New York.

Palmer, S. (2006) *Toxic Childhood*. New York: Orion.

Pearson, D. (2003) 'Resilience – giving children the skills to bounce back', Available at: www.voicesforchildren.ca

Penn (2007) *Penn Researchers Demonstrate Improved Attention with Meditation*. University of Pennsylvania.

Penn, A. (1999) *Targeting Schools*. London: Routledge.

Pert, C. (1997) *Molecules of Emotion*. New York: Scribner.

Pert, C. (2006) *Everything You Need to Feel Good*. London: Hay House.

Pintrich, P. R., Marx, R. W. and Boyle, R. A. (1993) 'Beyond cold conceptual change 'Review of Educational Research* 63(2): 169–99.

Posner, M. and Raichle, E. (1999) *Images of Mind*. Gordonsville VA: W.H.Freeman.

Posner, M. and Rothbart, M.K. (2007) *Educating the Human Brain*. New York: American Psychological Association.

Radiological Society of North America (2007) 'Autistic children may have abnormal functioning of mirror neuron system', *Science Daily*, 29 November.

Ramachandran, V. (2003) *The Emerging MInd – The Reith Lectures*. London: Profile.

Ratey, J. (2001) *A User's Guide to the Brain*. New York: Little, Brown.

Ratey, J. (2008) *Spark – The Revolutionary New Science of Exercise and the Brain*. New York: Little, Brown.

Rees, D. and Rose, S. (2004) *The New Brain Sciences – Perils and Prospects*. Cambridge: Cambridge University Press.

Reese, E. and Cox, A. (2000) 'Event memory in young children', *Applied Cognitive Psychology*, 14: 1–17.

Restak, R. (2003) *The New Brain*. New York: Rodale.

Riesenhuber, M., Jiang, X., Bradly, E., Rini, R., Zeffiro, T. and VanMeter, J. (2007) 'Categorization Training Results in Shape- and Category-Selective Human Neural Plasticity', *Neuron*, 53 (6): 891–903.

Robertson, I. (1999) *Mind Sculpture*. New York: Bantam.

Rose, S. (1992) *The Making of Memory*. New York: Bantam.

Rose, S. (2005) *The 21st Century Brain*. London: Jonathan Cape.

Royal Society of Arts (2007) *Drugs–Facing facts*.

Sample, I. (2007) 'The brain scan that can read people's intentions', *The Guardian*, 9 February.

Sapolsky, R. M. (2004) *Why Zebras Don't Get Ulcers*. New York: St Martin's Press.

Schacter, D. (2001) *Memory, Brain, and Belief*. Cambridge MA: Harvard University Press.

Schore, A. (1994) *Affect Regulation and the Origin of the Self*. Mahwah, NJ: Lawrence Erlbaum Associates.

Schore, A. N. (1999) Affect Regulation and the Origin of the Self. Lawrence Erlbaum Associates:

Schore, A. (2003) *Affect Dysregulation and Disorders of the Self*. New York: Norton.

Schwartz, J. and Begley, S. (2002) *The Mind and The Brain*. London: Harper Collins.

Seligman, E. (2006) *Learned Optimism*. New York: Vintage.

Seligman, M. (2002) *Authentic Happiness*. New York: Simon and Schuster.

Seung-Schik Yoo, H. P., Gujar, N., Jolesz, F. and Walker, M. (2007) 'A deficit in the ability to form new human memories without sleep', *Nature Neuroscience*, 10: 385–92.

Sharron, H. (1987) *Changing Children's Minds*. London: Souvenir.

Sheehy, R. (2005) 'Short term memory in infants', *Child Development*, 74.

Sigman, A. (2005) '*Remotely Controlled: How Television is Damaging our Lives*. London: Vemillion.

Siok, W., Perfetti, C., Jin, Z. and Tan, L. (2004) 'Biological abnormality of impaired reading is constrained by culture', *Nature* , 431: 71–6.

Smith, A. (2002) *The Brain's Behind It*. Edinburgh: Network Educational Press.

Smith, C. and Squire, L. (2005) Declarative memory, awareness and transitive inference, *The Journal of Neuroscience*.

Snowdon, D. (2001) *Aging with Grace*. London: Fourth Estate.

Sprenger, M. (1999) *Learning and Memory*. Alexandria, VA: ASCD.

Squire, L. and Kandel, E. R. (2000) *Memory From Mind to Molecules*. Gordonsville, VA: W. H. Freeman.

Stewart, W. (2006) 'British pupils among the least happy in Europe', *Times Educational Supplement*.

Sylwester, R. (1995) *A Celebration of Neurons*. Alexandria: ASCD.

Sylwester, R. (2004) Knowledge-based drug education. Connecting brain processes to school policies and practices. www.brainconnection.com

Thompson, J. (1988) *The Psychobiology of Emotions*. New York: Plenum.

Trainor, L. (2006) 'Musical training improves children's memory', *Brain*, September 2006.

Trevarthen, C. (1996) 'Lateral asymmetrics in infancy: implications for the development of hemispheres' *Neuroscience and Behavioural Reviews* 20 (4): 571–86.

Turner, J. (2000) *On the Origins of Human Emotions*. Stanford: Stanford University Press.

UNICEF (2007) Overview of Child Wellbeing. Available online at www.unicef.org/search/search.php?q=overview%20of%20child%20wellbeing (accessed 31 July 2008).

Usborne, S. (2007) 'Warp factor Zen', *Independent*, 28 August.

Vertes, R. and Siegels J. (2005) 'Time for the sleep community to take a critical look at the purported role of sleep in memory processing', *Sleep*, 28 (10).

Watkins, C. and Lodge, C. (2007) *Effective Learning in Classrooms*. London: Paul Chapman.

Wells, G., Bridges, A., French, P., MacLure, M., Sinha, C. and Walkerdine, V. (1981) *Language at Home and at School*. Cambridge: Cambridge University Press.

Wenner, M. (2007) 'Brain scans reveal why meditation works', Available at Live science.com

Western, D. (1999) *Psychology, Mind, Brain and Culture*. Chichester: Wiley.

White House, USA (2007) *Initiative on Educational Excellence for Hispanic Americans*. Washington DC: White House.

Wiggs, L. (2004) 'Children and sleep: Child and adolescent psychiatry report'. Oxford University.

Williams, J. R., Ramaswamy, D. and Oulhaj, A. (2006) '10Hz flicker improves recognition memory in older people', *BMC Neuroscience*, March 5, 7–21.

Williams, R. (2007) 'The brain rewiring and supercharging that makes Hamilton a master', *The Guardian*, 26 May.

Wills, C. (1995) *The Runaway Brain – The Evolution of Human Uniqueness*. New York: Flamingo.

Winn, M. (2002) *The Plug-in Drug*. Harmondsworth: Penguin.

Winston, R. (2003) *The Human Mind*. New York: Bantam.

Wolfe, P. (2001) *Brain Matters – Translating the Research to Classroom Practice*. Alexandria, VA: ASCD.

Wong, M. (2004) 'Sleep problems in early childhood and early onset of alcohol and other drug use in adolescence', *Alcoholism: Clinical and Experimental Research*, 28 (4): 578–87.

Zull, J. E. (2002) *The Art of Changing the Brain*. London: Stylus.

Index